Julian Durham

Hypnotized?

A Romance

Julian Durham

Hypnotized?
A Romance

ISBN/EAN: 9783744724968

Printed in Europe, USA, Canada, Australia, Japan

Cover: Foto ©Thomas Meinert / pixelio.de

More available books at **www.hansebooks.com**

HYPNOTIZED?

OR,

The Experiment of Sir Hugh Galbraith.

A ROMANCE,

BY

JULIAN DURHAM.

TORONTO:

The Ontario Publishing Company, Limited.

1898.

CONTENTS.

BOOK I.

THE EXPERIMENT IS CONCEIVED.

"The intuitive decision of a bright
And thorough-edged intellect."

—TENNYSON.

HYPNOTIZED?

CHAPTER I.

> "The feast is such as earth, the general mother,
> Pours from her fairest bosom, when she smiles
> In the embrace of autumn." —SHELLEY.

IT was autumn. The air was hot and still; the breeze which earlier in the day stirred lazily amid the trees had fainted in the glare of the setting sun that touched with its vivid rays the gorgeous tints of autumn's decaying splendour, turning each tree and shrub to golden red, whilst the common beyond glowed in the heat like an iridescent purple plain.

In the fields the men were harvesting the yellow grain. The hum of machinery broke softly on the ear as the barley swiftly fell before the reapers. It was drawing towards the evening of a day in early September, and shadows soon began to fall athwart the fields of swaying corn and low-lying pasture lands, where the white-faced Herefordshire cattle browsed contentedly, causing a tangle of sound to rise from their bells as they moved slowly to and fro. Myriads of grasshoppers chirruped where the flood of sunlight still remained, and the buzzing and whirring of many bright-winged insects made an infinite murmur in the still air, as the clouds, which rose slowly in the western sky, turned a glowing flame-colour, fit bed for the mighty God of Light to sink to rest upon. Gently the faint white mist stole up from the meadows down by the river; evening had come, that mystical hour when the long day of toil is over and a sense of rest lies upon the land.

All at once the stillness of the farm surroundings was broken by the clatter of teams as they came lumbering along the lane and approached the gate.

"Steady, m' beauties; whoa!" exclaimed one of the drivers, as the horses drew up suddenly; "whew! but it's been a powerful hot day, an' no mistake. Good evening, miss," he added respectfully, as a girl, who till now had been standing in the old-fashioned porch of the farm-house, came swiftly across the yard towards him.

"Bob," she said, and her fresh, young voice rang out clear and sweet, "Dad says you are to go down to the village after supper and tell Mr. Grey he can have those apples; and, Bob, I want you to nail up a shutter for me; I cannot reach it," and the girl smiled brightly at the driver as she made her request.

"Yes, Miss Ursula, I'll do it for ye, and welcome; and maybe ye'll tell the master as how I'll see Farmer Grey in the morning at the lower pasture, and won't that be time enough for them apples?"

As he spoke, the man finished unharnessing, and led

his horses off to the stable. Ursula slowly retraced her steps towards the house, humming softly meanwhile and swinging a large straw hat with one hand.

"I think I will go to-morrow," she pondered. "I might ride over in time for tea with Miss Wilkins. We could have a chat, discuss the whole matter, in fact, and then perhaps I shall know my own mind better. Miss Wilkins has such heaps of common sense, a quality Dad says I am sadly deficient in—but then he does not always mean what he says. Well, I'll go to Arleton to-morrow, and settle the question once and forever. Oh, Daddy!" as an elderly, broad-shouldered man came round the corner of the house, "are you ready for supper?" and the girl, linking her arm within that of her father, drew him towards the open-standing door.

Deepdene Farm-house was a large, rambling building; the windows, whose panes were diamond-shaped, looked out from under the overhanging eaves like shining eyes, as if they would fain gaze on the big, unknown world through the trails of ivy and honeysuckle which threatened to cover them. At one side of the house ran the yard, whilst a large garden lay behind, where sweet-smelling flowers grew in wild profusion, and narrow, box-edged paths lay between the rows of nodding dahlias and china-asters, which bloomed forgetful of the fact that autumn had come. Beyond stretched the grain fields and meadows, and winding through them the gleaming Arle flowed lazily on, singing its eternal song to the stones.

As Mr. Harlowe and his daughter sat down to their evening meal Ursula noticed that a shade of thought clouded her father's brow. He was a fine, robust-looking man of some five-and-forty years of age, and his rugged features wore a kindly look, not belied by the honest gaze of a pair of deep-set eyes. The lines of care, which a hard-working life had traced upon his forehead, added to rather than detracted from his appearance. His was a face to trust.

Belonging to that class of farmers who own their land through inheritance, and gain their position by means of education and self-respect, he was a man of unusual ability. As Ursula grew from babyhood to girlhood, all his ambition was centred in her, all the wealth of his deep affection was lavished on the child who brought brightness and joy into his lonely life. Mrs. Harlowe had died in the second year of their marriage.

"Ursula, lass, it's troubling me much, this matter of Polly Davis."

"Dear old Daddy, have not I told you a thousand times that I want nobody but you?"

"I know, my dear; still a companion would be good for you; you are too much alone, Ursula, and your cousin is a nice girl."

"She may be all you say, but I do not want her to come and stay here."

"With the winter coming on, and the long rainy days, you will find the house very dull," persisted her father, and the shadow on his face deepened.

"Now, Daddy, please do not insist on it. Give me your cup for some more tea."

"You know well enough that I cannot go against you, Ursula, in a question like this; but it is not right that you should be so much alone. You never seem to be friendly with the girls around here, and at your age you ought to have some women friends. It is not natural otherwise."

"Daddy," and she bent her head down so that he should not see the expression in her eyes, "I have Miss Wilkins; and as for the girls in the village—oh, cannot you understand—I do not care for their friendship; I"—but the burst of passionate feeling had died, and she ended quietly, "I am far happier alone."

Mr. Harlowe sighed. He knew well what she meant. Ursula had always held aloof from the companionship of the farmers' daughters in the vicinity; courteous and gentle, as she ever was towards all with whom she came in contact, a quiet reserve, a suspicion of hauteur, characterized her intercourse with those who, her equals in birth and surroundings, were, she instinctively felt, her inferiors in education and natural refinement.

"You had better hear what Miss Wilkins has to say, however, before you finally decide the question."

"Yes, I made up my mind to go and see her to-morrow. May I have Brown Bess?"

"Of course; do you not always get what you want, puss?"

"You are just a dear old Daddy," said the girl lovingly; "come, you have finished your supper, and it is too lovely to stay indoors this evening." So saying she drew him out into the soft, deepening twilight.

"I have some business to do to-night, child; it has been a busy day in the fields, and my head aches from the heat of the sun; but it is grand harvesting weather, so we must not grumble. Did you give my message to Bob?"

"I did; but he says that as he is going to see Farmer Grey to-morrow morning, it will be time enough then to tell him about the apples."

"Yes, that will do all right."

After a pause, during which the farmer lighted his pipe and took a few serious puffs at it, he inquired abruptly:

"Seen anything of Tom Scott lately?"

"No Daddy; at least," with a touch of evident embarrassment, "except yesterday. We met on the Arleton road, and he walked for a mile or so with me," and her truthful eyes looked straight at her father as she spoke.

"Umph!" grunted Mr. Harlowe. "I do not like

that fellow. An idle, good-for-nothing loafer; and none too sober, either, from all accounts."

"Really! Do you know anything about him—where he comes from, I mean?"

"No, lass, nor does anyone else around here. Robbins, at the Arleton Arms, told me he was a decent enough chap, but I do not like his looks myself."

"Perhaps you are a little hard on him, Daddy," said Ursula, who, though she disliked the man in question, began, womanlike, to defend him the moment his character was attacked.

"I know he is a hard drinker and is a gambler by profession; and I know also, Ursula, that I will not allow him to come into my house, or to associate with my daughter."

Having delivered himself of this speech, the farmer smoked away in silence for some time. Ursula, unaccustomed to hear her father express himself so tersely, was impressed in no small degree.

"I must go now, child; there are some accounts to be looked into before I can sleep to-night. Ah! if Polly were only here, you would not be left alone now," and with this parting shot Mr. Harlowe crossed the yard and disappeared among the out-buildings.

CHAPTER II.

> "Grace was in all her steps, heav'n in her eye,
> In every gesture dignity and love." —MILTON.

> "Her heart was light, and her soul was white
> As the winter's early snow."

URSULA walked on slowly past the hen-yard and down the garden path, each swaying motion of her figure betraying the grace of movement which was the outcome of her superb health.

Tall, more fully developed than is usual in a girl, who as yet half-child, half-woman, possesses the simplicity of the one with the fascination of the other, it seemed as if she had paused on the boundary line of her nineteen years to ask, "What is beauty? What is life?" so unconscious was she of her loveliness. And yet was she really lovely, this daughter of a race of sturdy farmers? Did not her charm rather lie in symmetry of form and a radiant freshness enhanced by the perfume of health? Her complexion was naturally fair, though slightly tanned by the sun; but a nose just too small, a mouth just too large, a chin just too firmly moulded —these were not the attributes of actual beauty. Still, no one is altogether perfect; and if Ursula's features were open to condemnatory criticism, at least the wealth of bronze-red hair, the curling lengths of which were gathered into a knot at the back of her shapely head, was a glory in itself. In her eyes lay the reflection of summer, but her mouth gave the key to the girl's nature. Self-control might veil her eyes, a touch of diffidence obliterate feeling from her other features, but her lips told the truth—they never lied: one glance at their proud or pained expression, one quick look at their quivering curves, revealed all.

Her heart, untouched by human passions, beat warm and true; for, living in a world of rustic tranquillity, there had been nought to disturb the even tenor of her existence, nought to stir the waves of feeling which lay beneath that calm exterior, or awaken to suffering and sorrow a nature whose untried depths might, if roused, prove as uncontrollable as a sullen sea.

With mind and soul as beautiful as the body which held them, she stood there, a "festival of beauty in the festival of life." No wonder she felt set apart from the girls of her own status; but, knowing well the impassable barrier of caste which separates the county from the country, she never attempted to cross the social Rubicon. Her one friend, Miss Wilkins, the mistress of a small school for girls in the village of Arleton, two miles distant from Deepdene Farm, had done much for Ursula. A strong mutual liking existed between the farmer's child and the gray-haired gentlewoman, which strengthened as the years rolled on and the girl grew to be one of her cleverest pupils.

Not of her teacher, however, nor yet of Polly Davis,

that estimable cousin to whose proposed visit she so strongly objected, was Ursula thinking on that September evening, as she strolled through the fragrant old garden. She was thinking of her lover. No strange thought for a young girl's mind to dwell on; and surely, as a rule, no unpleasant one either. Then, why the frown, the impatient gesture, as she uttered, almost involuntarily, the word:

"Detestible!"

"Yes, detestible!" she mused, "that he should have dared to look at me, to speak to me as he did yesterday. I could hate him, if I did not pity him. Poor Tom Scott! What was it he said? That he would turn over a new leaf, and work for me. How absurd the whole thing is. I wonder if Daddy guessed anything. I think not. Ah, well! The man is nothing, and never can be anything, to me."

And the stars came out, and the yellow harvest moon shone down on a sleeping world, but no one saw the dark form of a man, half-hidden by the laurels, whose white, sinister face was turned upward to where a ray of light shone through the chinks in the shutters of Ursula's window.

CHAPTER III.

> "Th' idea of her shall sweetly creep
> Into his study of imagination."
>
> —SHAKESPEARE.

IT was hot, very hot, and the country road stretched out, baked and dust-laden, as far as the eye could reach. Ursula Harlowe, returning from her visit to Arleton, jogged slowly along on Brown Bess, alternately fanning her hot face and flicking the tormenting flies off the tender-skinned neck of the horse. Her mission had been successfully accomplished; for, after much serious talk, Miss Wilkins finally gave the opinion that if the girl really so strongly objected to the advent of her cousin it would be better for Polly Davis not to visit Deepdene Farm just then.

As she trotted along the edge of the road, her mind still busy with the subject of the late discussion, Ursula almost unconsciously turned aside down a narrow track leading between two hedges full of honeysuckle and columbines and all the other bright-hued flowers which flourish in an English lane. Brown Bess, duly grateful for this change from the glare and dust of the highway, showed appreciation by dropping into an even walk and occasionally snatching at the leaves of the alder trees which overhung the path. A sharp turn and the road ran beside the rippling waters of the Arle, bordered on the other side by cornfields belonging to Mr. Harlowe's farm.

Suddenly, a man who had been fishing close by sprang up the bank just in front of the horse, and catching his foot in a network of brambles, fell heavily forward, the outstretched rod in his hand dealing Brown Bess a smart blow across the nose. It all occurred so rapidly that the girl, who had allowed the reins to drop listlessly through her fingers and her thoughts to wander far afield, with difficulty retained her seat at the sudden start and rearing of the animal under the shock of such an unexpected rap; but a soothing word, a firm grip on the snaffle, and Brown Bess quickly calmed down again, only giving vent to a snort of remonstrance, as a protest against such indelicate treatment.

"I beg your pardon. All the fault of my abominable carelessness," exclaimed Eric Desmond. "I am really awfully sorry," he continued, as, scrambling to his feet, he advanced, cap in hand, abject apology written on every feature.

"Oh, never mind; it is all right now," replied Ursula, smiling. "Do not mind about it, please; why, you could not help it. I do not for one moment imagine that you did it on purpose," with a touch of amusement in her tone.

"By Jove! I should think not; but I am a shockingly clumsy beggar, all the same, and deserve a good scolding for my awkwardness."

Meantime he had been patting the sleek neck of the

horse and noting in a vague way the well-set-up appearance of the rider.

"Oh, no, it was nothing; but see, your rod is broken; what a pity!"

"No one but myself to blame for that, anyhow," said he, stooping to pick up the article in question.

All reason for prolonging conversation seemed dead, and Ursula, becoming conscious that there was something distinctly unconventional in the interview, brought it to a close with a bow and a pleasant "good afternoon." Another moment and she was lost to sight round the corner of the road.

Eric turned to the river side, carrying his broken rod. He had been fishing with Sir Hugh Galbraith for a few days in Arleton, and now here was an end put to sport. It was very annoying, and gradually all thought of Ursula faded from his mind, as he sat down on a fallen log and commenced trying to patch up the damage. He could tie a fly better than most men, but to tie up a broken tip—that was another matter altogether.

"Hugh," he exclaimed, as the baronet approached him, "just see what I have done here—gone and broken this; so no more fishing for me to-day. Hard luck, is it not?"

"Yes; I saw you do it," replied his friend, quietly.

"You saw me! Then you must have seen the cause also."

"Or, rather, I saw the effect; a beautiful one too."

"What on earth do you mean?"

"I mean that of a lovely girl placed in a position to display her powers of nerve and control."

"Ah! I understand. Plucky child, eh?"

"Very," was the laconic response.

"Made a confounded ass of myself, falling like that and startling her horse."

"That girl is above the average," said Sir Hugh, thoughtfully. "Her figure, in its close-fitting habit, was perfect, and her face was full of something undefinable."

"What a queer chap you are," laughed Eric. "Always seeing what no one else notices. She is pretty, I grant you, but more than that—well, I did not perceive anything particularly striking about her."

Sir Hugh relapsed into silence; his thoughts, as if accelerated by the inaction of his tongue, whirled on and on in revolving circles; indistinct ideas were born, and nourished on the strength of a human purpose. The sight of Ursula Harlowe in the zenith of her girlish beauty had struck a sudden chord in his mind. The magnitude of it made him shiver; the very conception of it caused his brain to throb with alternate hope and fear. "It is possible," said intellect; "It is impossible," said common sense; "It shall be done," said ambition; and Fate laughed a long, long laugh.

The sun was sinking, and a tiny breeze ran hushing through the bending grass. Eric Desmond, having given up trying to mend his rod as a task not to be accomplished by his own unaided fingers, had flung himself down on the daisy-flecked turf and lighted a cigarette. Between the puffs he rambled on in a semi-disconnected sort of way to Sir Hugh, who, lost in engrossing thoughts, was at that moment far from being a dangerous enemy to the trout.

"Heigh ho!" yawned Eric, "back to London to-morrow I go, to groan and grizzle through a few more weeks of heat. No Scotland for me this year, worse luck. What would not I give to have a couple of days' good salmon fishing on the Tweed? To feel the pull, to play my line hither and thither, a long run, and then to land a fish of goodly size. That is sport, if you like."

"Yes, yes," murmured Sir Hugh, absently; but whether he had heard one word of Eric's dissertation, or even caught the drift thereof, was extremely doubtful.

"Fishing," continued the other, "is full of possibilities; that is why I love it so. Some day you may land a huge catch—who knows? The uncertainty is always there; for just as fish vary in size so do one's chances of catching them differ."

"Of course," assented his companion, "the difference is obvious." (He had evidently caught the last word only.) "She is very unlike the usual type of a society beauty."

"Great Scott! what are you talking about?" said Eric, sitting bolt-upright.

"Never mind me, old boy, I was thinking of other things, and got rather mixed up, that is all," replied Sir Hugh, suddenly realizing that his remark had not been *àpropos.*

Eric looked at him curiously. Could he still be thinking of that girl?

"As I was saying," he went on, "angling is a mystery. Therein lies one of its great fascinations. The fish live in one world, we in another; we are the catchers, they are the caught; but why sometimes they will bite and sometimes not, who knows? Temperature affects them, there is no doubt, and—"

"Eric, did you ever see such eyes? They were full of utter unconsciousness."

"Well, now you mention it, they generally are rather vacant."

"Vacant be hanged! Oh! Ah! yes—the fish, of course, yes—just so," and Sir Hugh broke into a peal of laughter. "Much fishing doth make thee mad, my friend," he continued. "It is an engrossing subject to its devotees, I know, but it tends to make them narrow-minded, and to think that every remark applies to it, and it alone. You will become egotistical, too, if you do not take care, for angling is the most selfish of all sports. Come, let us go back to the 'Arms.' I have had enough of this for one day."

The road led them past Deepdene Farm, where according to his usual custom, Mr. Harlowe was leaning over the yard-gate smoking a huge briar pipe. It was just that hour between day and evening when the glory fades from the sky, and the mantle of dusk falls over all things. There was a great stillness, too, lying heavily on the atmosphere; it seemed as if all living creatures had gone to rest early that night. The farmer heeded not the dying light, for his thoughts were busy. Into the mirror of days he looked, and saw—so far away it seemed now—the face of the girl-wife, of gentle birth, he had loved and cherished for two short years; a woman set on a pedestal and worshipped by the rough farmer who had won her. And the little child. He saw her also; she was growing up now; she would marry some day, but it must be a gentleman, a man of position, such as she had a right to wed. Crash! It was only a mirror, after all, giving back the illusions created by the longings of his own heart.

"Good evening," said Mr. Harlowe, as the two fishermen approached. "Had good sport, sir?" addressing himself more particularly to Sir Hugh.

"Yes, fairly good, thanks," drawled Galbraith in reply.

"I suppose one of you must be the gentleman who startled my daughter's horse this afternoon," suggested the farmer. "She told me all about it just now."

"I was the individual unfortunate enough to do so," said Eric, regretfully. "I trust Miss—"

"Harlowe," put in her father, as he paused.

"—Miss Harlowe is none the worse for her fright."

"Bless me, no; It takes more than that to upset my little girl. Ursula," as the subject of their remarks came out of the house towards them, "here is a gentleman—I do not know your name, sir—asking after you."

"My name is Desmond," said he, "and this is my friend, Sir Hugh Galbraith."

As Eric made this informal introduction, Sir Hugh turned, and looking full into Ursula's eyes, he instinctively took off his hat to her beauty.

"Miss Harlowe, I trust you have quite forgiven me," said Eric, turning to her as she stood by her father's side.

"Entirely," she replied; "please think no more of it."

Sir Hugh, meantime, had been quietly scrutinizing the girl from top to toe, and mentally sealing his compact with himself.

"Mr. Harlowe," said he, and the contrast between his present cordial tone and his late supercilious one was very marked, "I intend remaining in this neighbourhood for another week, and should be glad to learn something of the surrounding country. Could you furnish me with information regarding any antiquities worthy of note to be seen about here?"

"Certainly, sir, certainly. I shall be most happy to do so. If you could make it convenient to call to-morrow evening, I shall then be at liberty to tell you all I know on the subject."

Now such an appointment was precisely what Sir Hugh had in view, and, delighted to find that success had so quickly followed his manœuvre, he lifted his cap, and with an expression of thanks and a courteous "good night," left the farm premises in company with Eric.

That evening after supper Galbraith was very abstracted. A great scheme was slowly being perfected in his fertile brain, and so exhilarating was the thought of the experiment in which he was about to embark, that each moment he grew more certain of its ultimate success. By-and-by the fit of silence passed away, and he talked fluently to Eric as they sat in the parlor of the Arleton Arms. Politics, books, all the topics of the day came under discussion one after another, and about each of them he had some pertinent remarks to make. Desmond was both surprised and pleased. It was not often that the baronet displayed so much wit and volubility for his sole benefit.

"I really begin to believe that you are not only a truth-seeker, but a truth-speaker, Hugh," he said; "you seem in first-rate form to-night."

"Yes, I feel excited, I think, and when just a little bit elated, one is generally at one's best."

"Your command of language is almost as great as that of the immortal Webster himself," laughed Eric.

"For that compliment you deserve a seat in the

general Valhalla," replied Sir Hugh with mock politeness, and forthwith became so hilarious that Eric regarded him in astonishment, and glanced uneasily at the bottle of whiskey on the table.

"Not tipsy this time, old boy; see, it is more than half full still," said Sir Hugh, rightly interpreting his friend's quick look, and pointing to the suspected bottle. "As I told you I am excited, that is all; mere scientific exaltation I assure you;" and with another laugh he rose and went to his room.

CHAPTER IV.

> "You see the ways the fisherman doth take
> To catch the fish."
>
> "There are more things in heaven and earth...
> Than are dreamt of in your philosophy."
>
> —SHAKESPEARE.

"HOOKED him! By Jupiter!!"

"Pray do not let the excitement of the moment overcome you."

"My dear fellow, sarcasm is not your *forte*. Better let it alone," said Eric Desmond, who at the same time appeared quite unmoved by this attempted raillery on the part of his friend.

"I believe," he continued, "that my speckled gentleman will weigh a pound at the least; that makes seven fish altogether."

"A whole day's work in the broiling sun—result—seven trout. Query—is the result worth the labour?" and Galbraith puffed lazily at his cigarette, as he lounged on the river bank criticising his companion's skill.

"The fish are taking slowly to-day," replied the angler, who, having unhooked the last catch, and placed it in a creel slung across his shoulders, resumed his fishing, totally oblivious of the dissatisfaction expressed by Sir Hugh.

It was a glorious afternoon. A gentle breeze blowing up the water was just sufficient to hide the movements of the fisherman without impeding the true play of his line, and the place where Desmond had elected to fish that day was as lovely a trouting-place as the most epicurean angler could desire.

"Four o'clock, Eric," said Sir Hugh, looking at his watch, "and I am rapidly approaching a state of mental aberration caused by this infernal sun. Grilled brains are very nice, no doubt, but I am not desirous of having mine served on toast just yet."

"All right old boy; in half an hour I shall have reached the mill-dam—it is only a few hundred yards higher up—and then we will go back to the Inn."

"I cannot see why you are fishing up-stream in this heat; it may appear to you an idle question, but do you really prefer to have the sun blazing in your eyes?"

Eric laughed, a clear ringing laugh that was good to listen to.

"What a fool you pretend to be sometimes, Hugh," he said; "scoffer as you are at the idea of science in connection with sport, you must admit that to fish as I am doing has many advantages, one being that because a fish always lies with his head up-stream, and has no eyes in his tail, I see him before he sees me, consequently I can usually catch him."

"Your arguments hold water I suppose, but ye gods defend me from personally proving their truth," and

Sir Hugh, with an impatient shrug, blew a cloud of smoke from his Egyptian.

"It is true you know little of the real pleasures of fishing. Many a time, on a fine morning in May, when the water ran so low and clear as to necessitate the use of fine tackle with 'Blue Dun' or 'March Brown,' I have lured the wily trout from his hiding-nook and, given a good breeze blowing up-stream to favour the proper hang of the fly, have thrashed the water till my arm ached from wielding my rod." Eric Desmond's eyes sparkled at the recollection of days thus spent.

He was a tall, broad-shouldered man, handsome perhaps some people would have said, but—though bronzed by many a foreign sun, and possessing eyes of dark grey, which flashed with a strange lambent light under their heavy overhanging brows—he was striking-looking more by reason of the strength, both physical and moral, which characterized his face, than by any mere detail of feature. A large, square mouth betokened power, but when he smiled the sternness was forgotten in the sudden charm of fascination. Briefly, his face was masterful and his figure athletic. He could say "Damn," but could he say it at the proper time, and in the proper place? That was the question life and Eric Desmond would have to solve between them.

The only son of a wealthy squire whose landed property in Norfolk was the finest in that county,

Eric had been brought up under an easy rule. Eton and Oxford had turned him out, at twenty-two, a thorough Englishman, with a strong sense of right and wrong, and a strong will to back up that knowledge. A few years of travel and hardship in far-away countries had given ballast to his mind, and at thirty he was still, as he had ever been, a keen sportsman and an amateur philanthropist.

"Well, I am tired out," said Eric at length, flinging his creel and rod on the ground, and leisurely stretching his well-shaped limbs. "Whew!" with a gigantic yawn, "a long day's fishing under a broiling September sun is hard work."

"That is what I have been trying to impress upon you for the last three hours. You are too energetic, Eric, too bracing altogether; it is a pity that fortune has lavished the good things of this world so freely upon you."

"How so?" demanded Desmond.

"Why, my dear fellow, because should you lose wealth, position, all that makes your path in life so smooth now, I verily believe you would become one of the heroes of modern socialism."

"Bah! because I advocate a few commonplace theories, you would make me out a radical reformer."

"Oh, no! not at all," replied Sir Hugh, with a slight laugh; "at present I think you only quixotic, and your practicality very boring; but your fundamental power I admit, I might almost say envy," and the baronet's cold features lighted up with a brief flash of admiration for the noble strength of purpose which underlay his friend's character.

"There should be more hard work than leisure in life, just as there is more prose than poetry," said Eric. "To men of your stamp, the great questions of common work-a-day life bring no appeal. How should a cynical apostle of the ideal, such as you are, understand, or sympathize with the stimulating creed I believe in?" and the flickering light in Desmond's eyes betrayed his earnestness, as he continued: "While you seek in vain for that panacea which is to cure all the distempers of society, I devote myself to lessening the burden of human suffering by practical means. Why spend the best years of your life fondling your own chimeric ideals? Strike at the root of the evil!"

"In fact, be a second Don Quixote tilting at windmills," interpolated his friend.

"No, Hugh, only make your efforts coincide with the exigencies of the day. Give up being an aimless man, and concentrate your energy on some specific work."

"Look here, Eric, I concede that in a measure you are right; but why try to shatter my ideals? In the steady light thrown on them by years of experience, I see more clearly than ever that a man can be what he will."

"Granted," said Desmond, but he must cultivate a

singleness of purpose, which, for the time being, will banish from his mind all that is extraneous to the object he has in view, for success lies in concentration."

"My dear fellow, your arguments are like sledge-hammers, they strike hard; but, after all, are our views in truth so very dissimilar? We stand on neutral ground between the known and the unknown, a place full of undefined conditions. I uphold my ideal of mental science; you yoür ideal of physical work; but they are, nevertheless, both of them ideals."

"No, there we differ. In the pursuance of psychological research you strive after fantasmal results, and lose sight of the object of your existence, namely, to leave the world a nobler and happier place for your having lived in it; while in my creed all things must work in the direction of a tangible good which will benefit the community at large. My chief object is the amelioration of the universal law of suffering."

"When you talk of an object, you seem to forget that people with 'an object,' are usually called 'cranks.' No one takes kindly to them."

"Yet it is from amongst those who have no object in life that the great army of failures is recruited. Come now, Hugh, divest your mind for once of all transcendentalism, and step down to a solid basis. You are a man of twenty-eight, in the prime of life, and that you are capable of solving some of the deeper problems of that life I'll take my oath; why do you not work? Lay aside this dilettanteism which is sapping away your energy, and bravely face the stern reality of the evils you are now trying to remedy theoretically. Build up an ideal of duty, and build it on the rock of common sense."

"I am building up my life's work stone by stone, and I tell you, Eric, I shall succeed, even to the topmost pinnacle. But enough of this," as he threw away his cigarette with an impatient gesture; "the sun has nearly gone down, and we have to tramp back to the Inn before we can hope for supper."

CHAPTER V.

"The elements
So mix'd in him, that Nature might stand up
And say to all the world, 'This was a man!'"

—SHAKESPEARE.

"I SHALL have to run up to town the day after to-morrow, Hugh," began Desmond, as they swung along, skirting with rapid strides the fields of standing barley. How much longer are you going to stay here?"

"Don't know," was the laconic response; "perhaps a week, perhaps two; there is nothing to take me up to town at present"

"I should have liked a few more days of fishing in this part of the world, I must confess; but Wilson wants to see me about the Blackfriars scheme, and then, too, Sybil is lonely, I think."

"Probably, considering how much of your time you usually devote to her." Then, after a pause, Sir Hugh inquired, "When are you going to be married, Eric?"

"There is no date fixed yet for the wedding;" and as he spoke a sharp spasm of pain contracted his forehead. "Sybil has not made up her mind about it; very likely it will come off some time in the spring;" but he spoke with more hope than certainty in his tone."

"She is a deuced pretty girl." said Sir Hugh, "and so clever."

"Yes, too clever for a plain, matter-of-fact man like myself; but all the same I love her," he added simply, and the man who feared no living adversary lowered his eyes as he trembled at the thought of that perfect love which filled his heart.

"By the way, Miss Carlisle is a great pet of my aunt's," said Sir Hugh.

"Yes, Lady Brandram and Mrs. Carlisle are old friends, I believe, and Sybil dearly loves to go to Belgrave-square."

"The last time I met her there was at a 'musical crush,' such as Aunt Mary's soul delights in giving—a sort of menagerie party; and after some of the lions of the evening had roared in song, no doubt greatly to their own satisfaction, Miss Carlisle gave us a solo on the violin. By Jove! it was like the wind whispering among the trees, and made one think of summer, and sunshine, and—"

"Love," put in Eric, smiling.

"No; rather say a spirit-song."

"Sybil shows the touch of genius in her playing."

"Some day that girl will astonish London with her music. Mark my words, Eric, the world will ring with her praises yet."

"I trust not. As my wife, Sybil must give up all idea of a public career."

"But I thought she intended to study for the concert stage."

"Yes, she often spoke of so doing; but lately all necessity for earning her own living has been done away with, and when she is my wife it would naturally be impossible for her to embark on such a career."

Sir Hugh glanced up at his friend's face with a somewhat cynical smile. The calm, resolute air with which the latter disposed of his *fiancée's* future struck him as an assumption of arrogance on the part of the man towards one whom the light of genius had touched. Eric strode on with thoughtful mein. Galbraith's questions aroused an uncomfortable sensation in his breast, which for some weeks had lain there dormant; for, in spite of his cool assertion, he knew well that the strong force of his will had failed to bring Sybil Carlisle to look at things altogether from his point of view. Broad-minded and easy-going as he was by nature, there was one point on which he was inflexible. "Woman's sphere is home," he said. Woman's rights he abhorred; and though, on general principles, he entirely approved of the artistic world, he was one of those men who regard their own womanfolk as something to be kept quite free from any taint of bohemianism.

That Sybil should wish to shine in public was an idea unintelligible to him, and with a man's natural propensity to domineer he had told her that when she married him she must relinquish all thoughts of the stage. He had given her the best love of his life; not by any means the first love, but that full, entire devotion which a man can bestow only when the fritterings of passion are a thing of the past. In return for this he demanded her obedience and complete adherence. "I will not share you with music," he had said; "you must be all mine;" and she had temporarily acquiesced, for she was very fond of him.

That, however, was in the early days of their engagement, and now that six months had come and gone, Sybil began to show signs of returning allegiance to her art. Once or twice she ventured to speak of it to Eric, but each time he only answered: "Is not my love sufficient for you?" and half-ashamed she would keep silence, though the thought of her musical talent tormented her restless spirit.

The two men reached the commencement of the village street just as the fading beams of light gave a farewell kiss to the treetops, and the wind of an autumn dusk whispered a soft lullaby to the birds. There was an air of dreamy repose about the place; all nature's sweet curative influences seemed abroad in that quiet little Herefordshire village.

Within an incredibly short space of time, Sir Hugh and Eric Desmond were seated in the cheerful dining-room, partaking of a substantial meal, and later on, over a pipe and a good glass of whiskey and soda, they chatted about many things; old memories were awakened, and old friends discussed, until, by the time the tall clock in the corner struck eleven, and the two men rose to part for the night, Eric Desmond had forgotten all unpleasant impressions left on his mind by the conversation of that afternoon. And as he laid his tired head upon the pillow he thought, oh! so tenderly, of the girl he loved. "God bless her," he murmured, and fell asleep.

CHAPTER VI.

"He was exhal'd ; his great Creator drew
His spirit, as the sun the morning dew."

—DRYDEN.

SIR Hugh Galbraith was the descendant of a long line of ancestors. From a dreamy school-boy he had grown into a skeptical university student, and later on the skepticism merged into inquiry. Thus, at twenty-eight he was an ardent seeker after philosophical truth. Of a singularly elevated nature, the originality of his ideas was in a degree striking. Even people who did not understand him felt the power of his fascination, which, perhaps, lay partially in the fact that he never sought to convince those who differed from him. With that entire independence of thought which was his chief characteristic, Sir Hugh had been known to calmly set up his private opinion against the general dicta of older men, thereby causing an occasional startling revolution.

The commonly accepted forms of spiritualistic beliefs he considered painfully vulgar. They jarred on the transcendentalism with which he was saturated and, as he often averred, turned the sacred ideals of his creed into food for gossip amongst scoffers.

Exquisitely egotistical in all the minor relations of life, he bitterly resented the blatant mockery of his theories in which many materialists openly indulged, and, in consequence, as the years rolled on, grew colder and more reserved in his intercourse with the world, wrapping himself in a cloak of impenetrable cynicism.

It must be admitted that, with the arrogance of youth, he was often far too aggressive in his deductions, too eager to make all phenomena point toward the confirmation of his monistic philosophy; and yet there were seasons when, in utter loneliness of thought, he grew afraid. Would psychology lead him at last through the mists of doubt to the perfect knowledge of the one all-pervading Presence in which he believed? Would he through the spiritual reach the infinite? Thus, he by turns asserted and doubted, ever seeking and striving after truth, for God had given him a great soul.

So great was Sir Hugh's mental power that insensibly he controlled the minds of those who came in contact with him, and in the strength of this dominant force lay the secret of his influence over men and women. Silent, compelling, irresistible, was it purely intellectual, or was it that Unconscious Hypnotic power, of which scientists deny the very existence?

Tall and slight, he was of an essentially Saxon type, and his pale, clear-cut features betokened the man of breeding. A long, fair moustache half-hid his cold, handsome mouth; and eyes of steely-blue, fringed with peculiarly long lashes, glittered and scintillated, with a penetration in which there lurked something vague and awful, beneath a pair of straight eyebrows.

Anyone who had once heard Galbraith speak never forgot the tone of his voice. It was scarcely melodious, but the delicate timbre rang with a keen sweetness in the memory long after he had ceased to speak.

The present century has produced many men of this type. In the universal striving after something original, those minds, which, by hereditary refinement, are above the average, naturally imbibe the longing for perfection of some sort or another; and blindly stumbling on an old eternal truth they proclaim the discovery, forgetful that there is nothing new under the sun. What is it if their eyes have been opened to a tiny fraction of the things which have been and shall be? Are they not just one step nearer the knowledge of their own imperfection? When men learn to study nature, to love nature, and to believe in nature, they will then at last be near to the Knowledge of the Perfect.

A follower of Paracelsus, and an ardent believer in psychology, Sir Hugh was yet no practical expositor of hypnotism; he had always declined to take part in any *séances*, and further, though interested in experiment, disliked the flavor of charlatanism of which most hypnotic treatment smacked. Theoretically, he found all things possible; to prove them so practically, he never attempted.

CHAPTER VII.

"The intellectual power, through words and things,
Went sounding on, a dim and perilous way!"
—WORDSWORTH.

SEPTEMBER was seven days older. Such a lovely week it had been too, full of sunshine and warm-scented breezes. It was a period of deep interest to Sir Hugh; for, as day after day he went on steadily cultivating the society of Ursula and her father, his purpose grew more feasible in his eyes. Each time he saw the girl he became further convinced that in her lay buried the makings of a magnificent woman, such a one as would turn men's heads, and might, if she chose, place her foot on the very keystone of the social arch.

No word of all this had as yet escaped his lips, but the time was fast approaching when he must make the plunge and put all his hopes of carrying out his great experiment to the touch.

Days ago, Eric Desmond (who was entirely ignorant of Sir Hugh's contemplated scheme) had returned to London pavements, and now it was time for Galbraith to follow his example.

"I will stay only a little longer," Sir Hugh had said; yet there lay his portmanteau still empty. No signs of immediate departure were visible.

Often, during that week, he talked with Ursula,

trying to probe the depths of her nature, in order to ascertain how far she was fitted, mentally and morally, to be a test-subject for his contemplated experiment. Sometimes he thought he had fathomed her completely, when, lo! at a sudden turn she baffled him. Her child-like simplicity contrasted so curiously with her firm, unbending principles that occasionally she puzzled the man of science, by whose worldly standard she could not be measured.

"Miss Harlowe," he said to her one day, when their acquaintanceship was but three days old "who gave you that book I saw you reading yesterday?"

"Do you mean the translation of Goethe's 'Faust'?"

"Yes; where did you get it from?" he asked, interestedly.

"It belonged to my mother, I think," she replied.

They were walking along by the river, which flowed lazily between its banks as if too much overcome by the heat to hurry onward to where the great ocean awaited it, far beyond the distant purple hills. Sheltered beneath a large white umbrella, Ursula was bidding defiance to the sun, whose burning glances lay reflected on the broad, placid waters of the Arle, specked here and there with gaudy-hued flies that danced a perpetual tarantella on the bosom of the stream.

"Do you like the story?" asked Sir Hugh.

"Oh, no; it is dreadful, I think, and so sad," turning a sudden glance to him.

"And yet it is an every-day one," said he, calmly.

"Ah! no, no!" she replied, clasping her hands, as if imploring him to contradict that last statement.

He smiled. "It is true. Even you," with a touch of superciliousness, "cannot be entirely ignorant of all the sorrow that exists in the world."

"Perhaps you might with justice call me ignorant. I do not know much about the world, we are so apart from it down here in this little village; but," and she threw her head up with a proud gesture, "I am a girl and I know that girls are naturally good and pure and true, and that only in rare instances does such awful sorrow as Marguerite's come to them."

Sir Hugh was silenced for the nonce. Here was a verdict delivered by a simple country child, who did not hesitate to announce it as final. He felt the superiority was momentarily hers. The subject was a difficult one to touch on with a young girl, so he drifted somewhat away from the main point as he said:

"Sorrow and suffering come to all of us in turn. The story you were reading yesterday was only written; it could be re-written many times; but the story we live can only be lived once, and our actions once committed can never be recalled; the consequences of them must be endured to the end as best they can."

"It is not always our own actions that bring us trouble, but sometimes those of others. Marguerite suffered for the temptation to which she succumbed, but Faust was the real offender."

"Woman-like, you blame the man."

"I try to be just," she said, raising her unfaltering eyes to his, "and besides, you, at any rate, should agree with me; it is not manly to put the blame on a woman. I love my own sex," she continued with enthusiasm; "women are so brave; they struggle on through troubles as long as strength permits, hoping against hope, plodding bravely upward, and often they have much to bear."

"You are a staunch advocate," said he, with a swift intuition that she was telling him her inmost thoughts. "Women are usually good judges of each other in one particular only, that of pronouncing sentence."

"In what way?"

"Condemnatory, always."

"Who is unjust now?" with an arch smile; "you are giving voice to rank heresy. But why think of disagreeable things? Life is so sweet, so full of pleasure."

"And so I trust it always will be for you, Miss Harlowe; but to return to the original subject of our discussion; will you tell me why you think poor Faust so altogether in the wrong?"

"Because he was a coward," with flashing eyes; "he left her alone to bear all; oh! the piteousness of that lonelihood," and as she spoke the sympathetic tears rose slowly, and gathering, dimmed her sight. "A man should be strong," she went on in a monotonous undertone, as if compelled by some unseen force to utter aloud what was passing in her mind; "he should support and help a woman so that she may feel she can lean on his stronger nature, and find the rest she craves for in his sheltering arms. Should he be the one to throw her aside? Oh no! he should treat her as the chivalrous knights of old treated their queen. The other day I read a Canadian love-story—it was beautiful, and so happy, it was like real life,—far more so than that sad tale of Faust and Marguerite."

Sir Hugh removed his eyes from her, and unconsciously she stopped speaking.

Upon these two beside the river a silence had fallen, a weird music arose from the depths of the waters, a few withered leaves rustled past them, wind-swept across their path. How full of noble thoughts was this girl, pondered Galbraith, so unspotted by the mildew of society, so healthy-minded in her belief in a creed of universal honour. In the world into which he dreamed of introducing her, *bon gré—mal gré*—she would be a revelation. Her low, soft voice, one of woman's greatest charms, aroused him from his reverie.

"You do not think ill of all women, do you?" she questioned anxiously; "you are so good yourself, you must know that others are good also."

"Miss Harlowe, your remark is not only original, it is unique. I do not pretend to be—I mean (seeing her look of bewilderment), it is not *fin-de-siècle* to be good—one must study to be amusing, witty—but good—the thirst for novelty at any price has not yet demanded that of society."

The next moment he regretted his highly-spiced banter. The adorable modesty of her mind caused his remarks to glance off, leaving it unharmed; but one look at her puzzled face had been enough to silence his graceless speech.

"I beg your pardon," he said humbly, "my words were senseless, but do not think too much of me. I am only a very ordinary sort of man."

"You are my friend," she said, gently.

"Thank you for that gift of your friendship," he replied, and stooping, loyally kissed her small, sunburnt fingers, thereby causing a rosy glow to mount swiftly into her cheeks.

The strong interest with which Sir Hugh had from the first inspired Ursula Harlowe was rapidly developing into something more intangible and powerful. To him she was a purely psychological study—to her he appeared the embodiment of all that was great and noble; and while Galbraith was too absorbed in his experiment to notice the strange control he at times unconsciously exercised over the girl, she, on her side, was too simple-minded to realize the meaning of that strong, compelling power which insensibly dominated her.

They talked incessantly of this thing and that, often

disagreeing, for Ursula could hold her own in any argument where her natural instincts sufficed; but slowly, yet surely, Sir Hugh was opening up before her new fields of thought—comparisons of town and country life, glimpses of brilliant society as contrasted with the trivial monotony of her daily round—into such channels did he lead her mind. That Galbraith never once thought of her as a loving, loveable girl, but only as a beautiful creation, was as true as it was strange. To him she was simply *une nature.*

CHAPTER VIII.

Cut prejudice against the grain.

—TENNYSON.

ONE morning while Sir Hugh was seated at breakfast, engaged in the demolition of unlimited toast and marmalade, the waiter came and laid a letter beside his plate. Having glanced at the familiar handwriting, he eagerly ripped open the envelope and began to read its contents. It ran thus:

Belgrave-square, September 15th.

DEAR OLD HUGH:—

But perhaps I ought not to call you so any longer. Why! you are nearly thirty! and must be verging on that indefinite age when to be called old is apt to be regarded as an insult! What on earth is keeping you in the wilderness so long? Mr. Desmond called on us three days ago and told me you were fishing; now my dear boy, such sport is no doubt very charming, but truly I think you must have other fish to fry than "ye speckled trout," or Herefordshire would not have claimed you for its own so long, especially as you are the laziest of anglers.

You will see from the heading of this letter that I am staying with Aunt Mary. The dear soul adores me as much as ever, and I am having a rattling good time of it, no end of theatres, and flirtations, but alas! people are still scarce in Mayfair, and a ball is a thing of dreams only.

Marmaduke is in town and as idiotic as ever. Really Bedlam should be his abode during his sojourn on this terrestrial globe; his awful puns and ghastly attempts at playing the court-fool make me sick. Do come home, Hugh. Aunt was saying only yesterday how she missed you. The dear old lady is quite well, and chaperones me everywhere most religiously.

Sybil Carlisle dined with us last night, and, of course, Mr. Desmond also. How devoted they are to one another. I do not believe I could ever fall in love with anybody like that. Change is what I like, for as soon as an individual person grows specially attached to me, in that instant he becomes a bore. As long as the world loves me, and I love all the world, (quite platonically you understand), I am perfectly happy; but then, why should I not be so? I never get up till noon, nor do an earthly thing that does not please me. *Voilà tout!*—A truce to moralizing, however.

I must not forget to tell you about Marmaduke's latest atrocity. It was at tea-time he perpetrated it. I had remarked to him casually, that the world was no better a place for his temporary habitation thereof; that, in fact, he had lived in vain. "I never lived in vain," he replied; "I always lived in England." Now was not that silly? And he actually expected me to laugh. But I must say, even Marmaduke at his worst (and he can be very appalling) was preferable to our other visitor, Mr. Chaytor, who is a good young man, and should meet Sarah Grand. She might appreciate him. I do not.

Fare-thee-well, and for mercy's sake hurry up and come home to

Your affectionate cousin,

BETTY.

"What a little scatter-brain she is to be sure!" mused Sir Hugh, as he folded up the sheets covered with Lady Betty Mornington's hieroglyphics. "A dear little scrap of humanity all the same. Ah! my pretty cousin, I am very fond of you; your smile is like a sunbeam in a shady corner, your laugh an echo of joy itself. You are right, I must go home,—and my great purpose,—that must be put in process at once. If I succeed in this grand experiment, I shall have disproved a time-worn theory, and given to the world of society a queen worthy to reign over it. The science of transplantation, that is what it is; and you, beautiful Ursula Harlowe, shall flourish in a richer soil than that in which you have hitherto grown. You shall be transplanted from the field to the hot-house, in order that you may ripen to perfection, and the transplanter shall be Hugh Galbraith."

As the last morsel of marmalade-bestrewed toast disappeared, he pushed back his chair, and, with determination written on every feature, started for Deepdene Farm. It was in one of the corn-fields, now full of stacked sheaves, that Sir Hugh found the farmer that morning.

"Mr. Harlowe," he said, "may I have a few words with you? It is my intention to return to Town by the afternoon train, and there is an important matter I should like to discuss before leaving."

"Certainly, Sir Hugh. I'd enjoy a bit of rest myself, and if you'll come across the field to yonder trees, we can have our talk in comfort."

Through the blazing sunshine they walked together, where the dusty beams of light fell with intense brightness, and even the grasshoppers seemed to have lost the strength to chirrup and hop.

"I have a proposal to make to you," began Sir Hugh, after a few silent puffs at his cigar, and his voice sounded steady and calm, in spite of the great anxiety which filled his mind. "It is an unusual one in itself," he went on, "and calculated to lead to many changes, but should you agree to it, I shall assume all responsibilities and pledge my honour to fulfil the obligations it will entail upon me; in short, what I am about to ask you to do is to allow me to launch your daughter into fashionable London society."

It was over. The plunge had been made, but, even as he paused, a tiny chill crept down the baronet's spine and a sense of choking threatened to overmaster him.

"What!" exclaimed the farmer, his face a study of astonishment and wrath, "my little Ursula!! I think, sir, you must be either mad or dreaming to suggest such a thing. Your words are almost an insult. How do such as you dare to propose this thing?"

"I fear I have been somewhat hasty, Mr. Harlowe, and my words were blunt, but," he went on haughtily—for by this time he had regained perfect self-control—"the means I intend to use in the accomplishment of this scheme are above suspicion."

Surprise and indignation had rendered the old

man momentarily dumb. He merely nodded, and Sir Hugh continued:

"What I propose is that you confide your daughter to the care of my aunt, a lady of middle-age, and established position in London, and that under her care Miss Harlowe shall make acquaintance with the world of fashion. Your daughter is beautiful, far too beautiful to bloom in the obscurity of a country village. She is superb in her youth and health, and in Town would be an acknowledged queen."

"Your words are bold ones, Sir Hugh. Ursula is pretty, but among the fine ladies of society she would be out of place."

"No, no; I have watched her during our short friendship, and with money at her command, and a suitable chaperone, she would have all the world at her feet."

"She is only a little country girl, and quite unversed in all those things which form part of the education of the daughters of nobility. I would not have her sweet nature shamed by the knowledge of its unconventionality."

"Say rather that she is one of nature's gentlewomen," replied Sir Hugh quietly; and long afterwards in the light of later events he remembered the strange smile which for an instant hovered round the corners of Mr. Harlowe's mouth, as the latter responded:

"True, she is in every respect a gentlewoman. All

the same," he continued, "it is impossible, I tell you, absolutely impossible. I will not listen to any such foolish ideas. You may be honest in your intentions," with a keen, sidelong glance at Galbraith, "but this thing you suggest is absurd, and even if you ever succeeded in gaining my consent, think of the aunt you mentioned; would she be willing to receive a girl of whom she knew nothing, who was an utter stranger to her?"

"I am confident that my aunt would not refuse to receive Miss Harlowe," replied Sir Hugh. Lady Brandram had always complied with any demand he made on her good nature, and such a simple thing as launching a lovely girl into London life,—why she would jump at the idea of it, he thought. Which notion only served to show how much Sir Hugh had yet to learn of the ways of women.

"Once for all, I must decline your proposal, sir. Ursula is not suited to a grand life, and then the expense—I am not a rich man, and have no money to throw away on foolishness."

"Do not let that stand in the way," urged Sir Hugh. "My aunt is wealthy; Miss Harlowe should want for nothing." This was a distinct perversion of the truth; Sir Hugh was enormously wealthy—his aunt was not.

"It cannot be, sir, I am sorry, but it cannot be," and Mr. Harlowe rose as if to put an end to the discussion.

The young man betrayed no sign of defeat.

"Well, farmer," he said, "let us leave the matter in abeyance for the present. Perhaps some day you may change your mind."

"I think not; but I thank you, sir, all the same, for your kindness in thinking of my little girl. I believe you mean what you say, and would treat her honestly, but I could not spare her,—she is all I have to live for."

While this conversation was taking place, Mr. Tom Scott was also improving the shining hours by trying to secure an uninterrupted talk with Ursula. The sharp rebuff she administered to him some days before had not had the desired result, for he absolutely declined to accept his *congè*. Tom Scott was a spare man, clean shaven, with lips thin and cruel, and tortured at the corners by a wretched smile which showed weakness rather than strength, in that the reserve force was being constantly called into play. Gambler, tuft-hunter that he was, any good that had not been entirely crushed out of his nature rose to the top since love for Ursula Harlowe had touched him. Love is a powerful agent, and can even change a man's whole nature under given circumstances, but, unfortunately, all it had done for Tom was to temporarily gloss over his low cunning with a veneer of honesty. Since her refusal to listen to his wooing, the man had dogged her footsteps day after day, watched her, spied on her actions, and consequently soon became aware of the frequency of Sir Hugh Galbraith's visits to Deepdene.

To love is to know the meaning of the word rival;

therefore Scott hated the baronet. Once more he pleaded with Ursula, and once more she firmly refused him.

But the man declined to accept her reply as final, declared he would wait for months, years if need be—that time which held all things might yet hold the gift of her love for him,—perhaps some day the constancy of his affection would win her.

A great passion for her beauty had taken possession of him, and win her he would, or, said he, if he failed it should not be because another man succeeded.

Tom had not dared to again enter the farm house, but was talking to Ursula at the garden gate when Mr. Harlowe and Galbraith came strolling up the lane. At this unexpected sight the farmer was furious, whilst Ursula, conscious of a constraint in the air, advanced with a friendly smile to greet Sir Hugh.

"Good morning," she said. "Come under the trees and rest; or, as I am going to feed the chickens, perhaps you will help me."

"I shall be delighted," replied Sir Hugh, "but please remember I strongly object to any violent exertion on such a hot day."

"You have evidently not forgotten your chase after Brigham Young," laughed Ursula.

"I should think not. That noble head of the barnyard proved one too many for me, and if he escapes to-day, I bar being made to pursue him."

"That is right, Sir Hugh; don't you let my little

girl impose on you," said the farmer, who, during the above conversation, had been standing irresolute as to what course he should take. "Well, Mr. Scott," he continued, when Ursula and her companion had walked off in the direction of the house, "may I ask what brings you here?"

"I just looked in for a few minutes to see Miss Harlowe, farmer, but now that I find she is otherwise engaged," with a vindictive sneer at Galbraith's retreating back, "I'll say good morning."

"Just so! say it once for all," blurted out the irate old man, "I'm pretty plain-spoken, and you are not my sort; so we'd best part, and be done with it."

"You think that I am not good enough for you, that I am not such a swell as that chap yonder, with a handle to his name, curse him!"

"It is no business of yours whom I choose to admit to my house, but I'd have you understand, Tom Scott, that you, at any rate, are not welcome."

"Stop a moment, farmer. You despise me—I see can it—but I'm not altogether a bad sort; and if you treat me squarely, I'll work for your daughter."

"That you'll not get the chance of doing; Ursula shall never marry a man who is a gambler and a drunkard. You've forced me to say it; and now—go."

Scott's eyes gleamed with a savage light at the old man's rough words.

"By gum!" he mentally ejaculated, "I'll give him one for that."

"I'm going," he added aloud, "but let me tell you this: you've refused to listen to a man who would make your daughter an honest wife. Take care; those kind," indicating Sir Hugh, who was still visible in the distance, "do not marry country girls."

"Hold your tongue, you insolent scoundrel," roared Mr. Harlowe. "How dare you speak to me like that. I know very well that you are after my lass, and I know I'd sooner see her dead than give her to the likes of you. So don't let me have any more philandering here."

"You go too far, Mr. Harlowe. Every man has a right to make love to a woman who is free; and if I tried to win your daughter, I did so openly and and honestly."

"Look here," said the farmer, whose blood was now at boiling-point; "you leave my place this instant, and never show your damned face here again. Go!"

"But—"

"Go!" he repeated.

"Perhaps some day my turn will come," snarled Scott, "and when it does—"

But Mr. Harlowe had turned on his heel, and was half way up the garden-path, so the threat, whatever it might have been, was lost upon him.

CHAPTER IX

> "And when the stream
> Which overflowed the soul was passed away,
> A consciousness remained that it had left
> Deposited upon the silent shore
> Of memory, images and precious thoughts
> That shall not die, and cannot be destroyed."
>
> —WORDSWORTH.

MR. HARLOWE was worried, and he was very angry. As far as Tom Scott's outrageous proposal was concerned, that was all settled and done with; but this other matter,—this proposition of Sir Hugh Galbraith,—it troubled him not a little. When the baronet first spoke of the scheme, the farmer had been seriously annoyed, but as he thought over the subject, doubts began to arise in his mind. Was he quite justified in denying to Ursula all chance of rising in the world? If this aunt of Sir Hugh were really willing to take charge of her, why should she not enjoy all the pleasures and advantages of such a life?

But then there was another side to the question. Mr. Harlowe was no fool, and he wanted to know some good and valid reason for the deep interest Sir Hugh took in the girl. Had the man shown signs of being in love with her, it would have satisfactorily explained affairs; but though he sought her society on every occasion, there were no further indications that he entertained any deeper feelings towards her than those of friendship, and the farmer knew very well that ordinary friendship does not, as a rule, lead a man to propose such a scheme as the one laid before him by the baronet.

Tom Scott's remarks also lingered unpleasantly in his mind, and it was largely owing to his inability to fathom the motives of Galbraith, that Mr. Harlowe declined so firmly to listen to his ideas.

"There is a screw loose somewhere," thought the old man; but had he been told the real reason why Sir Hugh urged him to let Ursula go to London, he might have been still more mystified, for that a man should plan, and carry out such a great undertaking, solely for the sake of experiment, would have been incomprehensible to his rustic mind.

Finally, he determined to let the matter rest. Sir Hugh was to him a complete enigma, for Galbraith had no small talk, no commonplaces; then too, his somewhat rigid pose disconcerted the genial farmer, and made him mentally call the baronet "that cast-iron man," at the same time confessing that he could make no progress in conversation with him. How it came about that Ursula and Sir Hugh were such great friends was a constant puzzle to her father; with the girl Galbraith seemed quite *en rapport;* but when he was with Mr. Harlowe, conversation flowed with difficulty; it was a case of speech *frappé.*

And Ursula, what of her? Had she been interrogated as to whether she liked Sir Hugh or not, she would have replied "yes" unhesitatingly, and would then have paused—and said nothing more. She was happy in his society, and the whys and wherefores did not matter yet.

"Chuck, chuck, chuck!" called Ursula softly, and from far and near, in answer to her welcome, the clucking army of fowls came scrambling to her from every corner of the yard.

"They are almost as greedy as the proverbial lawyer," laughed Sir Hugh.

"And so mischievous too. You have no idea what a lot of damage they do in the garden, if by any chance they get loose there. Even Don cannot up-root the flower-beds as satisfactorily as they can,—Oh! quick, quick, there they go making for the gate. I,—you,—somebody must have left it open. Hurry, hurry, do not let them get through," cried Ursula frantically; for, finding that the generous dinner provided for them had come to an end, with true fowl-like ingratitude the whole mass of cocks and hens at once roamed off in search of pastures new, and seeing the garden-gate open, with one accord they made a rush to enter the coveted paradise.

Away flew Sir Hugh, calling loudly to the now excited army, who, legs flying in all directions, and tails half-fanned, were running as fast as nature permitted. But he proved too quick for them. Bang!—the gate was shut, and away went the mob of scurrying bipeds, some of them almost flying in Ursula's face as she came up in hot pursuit.

"Thank you so much," she panted breathlessly, as she fanned herself with her hat, an ancient one and somewhat devoid of brim. "What wretches they are; but, thank goodness, you won the day."

"Victory unquestioned," replied he; "a bloodless one it is true, but decisive nevertheless. May I sit down here for a few minutes?"

"Surely, yes. A victor deserves his well-earned rest. What a chase it was! Ha, ha, ha!" and the laughter came rippling out, as she leaned her head back on her clasped hands, and looked up at Sir Hugh. "You did not expect to have such an exciting run, did you?"

"No, I should think not; but, tell me, are you always so gay? Laughter seems so near to you, that one would imagine you were never sad."

"I am happy," she replied thoughtfully.

"You are fortunate," he said; "few people in this world can say that."

"But why?" she questioned, somewhat surprised. "I love the farm, and I have Daddy who adores me. Of course I am happy,—at least generally," with a slight hesitation in her voice.

"You love the country?" queried Sir Hugh.

"Oh yes! I have always lived in it. Once Daddy took me to Hereford for a week; it was lovely,—how I did enjoy it. The shops, the big houses, and the Cathedral; have you ever been there?"

"Yes," once, long ago. So you liked the place?"

"It was great fun seeing everything; but somehow it tired me. I was glad to get back to Arleton."

"But the town, and all the people,—did you not like the stir and bustle of a large place?"

"At first I did, but afterwards it seemed to make me feel lonely. You see I knew nobody."

"Yet you are not lonely here."

"Sometimes I am. Sometimes," turning her eyes to his, "I am fearfully lonely."

"Would you like to have more friends,—the companionship of other girls?"

She was looking away from him again,—far away across the meadows to the blue hills beyond, and as she answered, there was something in her voice betokening dissatisfaction.

"I do not care for girls much, at least not those about here. I do not quite know what it is I want. As a rule I am busy, but when Daddy is away, and the long evenings come, then, when there is no one to talk to——"

"That is the time you are sad, is it? Yet there can be no corner of your life wherefrom to call forth a troubled recollection."

There was a short silence, then Sir Hugh continued abruptly: "You look tired; you must not stay here any longer in this hot sun. Come," holding out his hand to her with a touch of decision, "let us go to the summer-house over there, and let me get you a glass of water."

Ursula rose mechanically and followed him. Somehow this quiet, cynical man had gained a curious ascendency over her. It even gave her pleasure to obey him, and now she was like a weary child, doing as she was bidden, with unquestioning faith.

Inside the summer-house coolness reigned supreme, and the girl, sinking on to the mouldy old seat, was thankful for the change. It was so silent there, everything suggestive of movement or activity so far away, that with a delicious sense of indolence she leaned back and gave herself up to a feeling of rest.

Silence, however, cannot be eternal, and presently she looked up to find Sir Hugh regarding her intently. Instinctively she shrank backward, and her very soul seemed to cry out, "Let me alone! Let me go! Struggle, struggle, struggle! Ah!"

"Well," said Sir Hugh interrogatively, "do you feel cooler now?"

Cool,—she was cold as if an icy wind had touched her heart. With a sense of shame the girl deliberately drew herself up and, flushing, replied:

"Yes, it is better here. I was only thinking that ——"

"What?" questioned he, smiling.

"That I was tired." And in truth she was so.

"I would leave you now, but I go to London this afternoon, and it is hard to cut short our last chat together."

For a moment she was dumb, and Sir Hugh lost

himself in a dispassionate study of her expression. What was it her face portrayed? A vivid crimson had sprung into her cheeks, a look that might be termed shy crept into her eyes,—then how pale she grew.

"To London! You are leaving Arleton then?"

"Yes, I must go to-day." He was watching her keenly.

"I am sorry; but you will come back soon?" turning her face to his, as though waiting for an answer.

"Perhaps; still, who knows, we may meet in London first." Ursula smiled. "No chance of that, I think. Why, London is so far away, and I," with a sigh, "so seldom leave home. Only once Daddy took me away, that time I told you of, when we went to Hereford."

"To be sure; but you would like to go to some great city, would you not?"

"I do not think so. You see, I should miss so many things—my horse, for instance."

How unsophisticated she was on some points. Anything so *naive* and fresh had not often come within his knowledge.

"You could ride even in London," he rejoined, "there is always the Park."

"But that must be very stiff, not like a good gallop across our dear old fields. Look at the common over there; that is where to ride, with the wind blowing fresh on one's face, and the spring of the elastic turf under foot, to ride and ride on through the heather and broom, to drink in big draughts of the flower-sweet air, or to feel the coming storm sweeping on towards you, to hear the fearful stillness, the pause before the thunder breaks, and then, to race home with the great drops pattering on your face. A wild gallop, as your horse makes long, irregular swerves, and the thudding throb of his hoofs keeps time in the glorious flight!"

Unconsciously she stood up, and threw out her arms with a gesture of freedom. Her eyes were sparkling with excitement, not so much emotional as the outcome of exuberant youth, to the charm of which no man is ever insensible.

"I should be smothered in a town," she said.

"But have you ever thought of the other side of the picture? Of the balls and the opera, and all the pleasures you would have?"

"No, I should not enjoy them, I should be too much afraid. I could not bear to know that not one familiar face was there to greet me."

"You forget; I should be there."

"You!" with a start, "Oh yes! I forgot you are going back to-day," and her voice sank with the last word. She had crushed some blossoms in her hand, and was looking at them listlessly, as one might regard some remote question.

"Tell me, would you feel afraid if I were there to help you?" He was looking at her again, and once more she felt the strange, awful domination of his gaze.

"I should never be afraid with you," she said, in a dazed sort of way, as though compelled to answer him with the bare truth.

"Of course not," he replied, carried away by her words, and ignoring the strained manner in which they were spoken. "Still it is only fancy after all; you will stay at home, and I shall go to London; but in a week, perhaps, I am going to run down here again."

He had removed his eyes from hers, and she breathed more freely.

"You are coming back, then. I am so glad."

Galbraith might have made some kindly rejoinder, but at that instant the sound of Mr. Harlowe's voice reached them. Another moment, and the farmer appeared round the rhododendrons.

Sir Hugh made a movement towards the gate.

"Good-bye, Mr. Harlowe," he said; "good-bye, Miss Ursula," and the intensity of his regard compelled her at once to turn her eyes to his. She laughed faintly.

"Good-bye," she said, and so absorbed was the girl in the thought of his going, that she did not notice that her mirth received no acknowledgement. Tremulous tears rose in her eyes as she watched the baronet depart.

He was gone,—and with a slight shiver she turned to enter the house.

Down the dusty road tramped Galbraith, thoughts thronging in upon him in tumultuous riot. Hope reigned triumphant in his heart. He must, he would succeed, in spite of Mr. Harlowe, or rather in conjunction with him,—for a Macchiavellian idea had suddenly struck him,—only a few rounds in the game had as yet been played, and he still held a trump card. Would it take the odd trick? He thought so. At any rate it should be played out quickly.

"Hullo! what is the matter?" he exclaimed, as a man suddenly met him face to face, and, standing in the middle of the road, attempted to bar the way.

"I want a few words with you, Sir Hugh," replied Tom Scott, for it was Ursula's disfavoured lover who thus tried to stop him.

"All right, but be quick about it, for I have a train to catch. What is it you want?"

"Don't be in such a hurry, my fine gentleman," answered the other, "what I have to say concerns Ursula Harlowe. Ah!" as Galbraith paused, "that fetches you, eh?"

"Come, drop this insolence, and say what you have to."

"Very well. It is this. I love that girl, and I intend to stop anyone else spooning on her. Do you hear?"

"I hear right enough, but I cannot see that it is any of my business."

"Oh no! can you not? Well, let me tell you then that I know your little game, and it won't work; see?"

"No, I do not see. If you are under the impression that I am in love with Miss Harlowe, I will tell you this much, that you are mistaken; but beyond that I decline absolutely to discuss her, or any other lady, with you."

"But if I insist on knowing what you do mean, why you go there so often, and why, ——"

"Oh! Go to the deuce!" said Sir Hugh, and he walked off across the fields leading to Arleton."

CHAPTER X.

> " Friend, when first I looked upon your face,
> Our thought gave answer each to each so true,
> And either lived in either's heart and speech."
>
> —TENNYSON.

THE stars shone clear, and the wind was hushed. In the distant woods some night-bird sang, in melancholy strain, a serenade to the sleeping flowers on whose folded petals dew-drops glistened and scintillated in the moonlight. The heavy perfume of *Gloire-de-Dijon* roses came in to Ursula, through the open window, where she sat dreaming in the big arm-chair and idly toying with a tiny kitten which lay curled up in blissful content on her lap.

Mr. Harlowe was leaning against the window frame. He had made up his mind to tell Ursula about Sir Hugh Galbraith's proposition, not thinking it right that she should be kept entirely ignorant of what had passed on the subject, yet it was with a certain amount of trepidation that in his habitual straightforward way he finally told her the whole truth.

Surprise, consternation, and then a great wonderment swept over the girl. She had the charm of being perfectly natural, and had, moreover, never learned the necessity for concealing her feelings; so, frankly and without constraint, she in return told her father of many things which had not hitherto come within his knowledge—of all her longings for a wider sphere, a fuller acquaintance with the world. At first the man was thunderstruck, as she thus poured out her heart to him, but when he realized that it was all very vague and that for the present she had not the slightest wish to leave home, he again grew satisfied that he had acted for the best, and was much relieved to learn that Ursula entirely approved of his decision.

Late on into the night she sat up thinking over all that her father had told her. Long she pondered on Galbraith's strange proposition, and what its ultimate consequences would be if she ever acceded to it; but, as in a dim manner she thus speculated on these possibilities, never for one moment did the girl imagine how soon they were to become realities.

One theme ran through all her thoughts. Sir Hugh was coming back—he had said he would return in a week. "He will come, he will come," was the glad refrain that mingled with her dreams. "He will come," whispered the moon-beams, as they trod their silver pathway, folded in a tender veil of mist. "He will come," echoed the trees, whose topmost branches were trembling in the air that stirs before the dawn. Ah! happy exuberant youth! so full of hope and joy and love! God forgive those who crush your fresh sweetness, and poison your trusting truth-white soul!

CHAPTER XI.

> "Society is now one polished horde,
> Formed of two mighty tribes, the Bores and Bored."
>
> —Byron.

At five o'clock in the afternoon, the tinkle of silver spoons as they clash against the cups, and the faint aroma of tea and hot cakes which pervades the atmosphere of the drawing-room, is ever welcome. Lady Brandram was always at home at that hour, much to the satisfaction of her large circle of acquaintances, who knew they were sure of a welcome, and a cup of orange-pekoe, should they drop in at her house in Belgrave-square after a round of shopping, or that even more exhausting process, a series of dull duty-calls.

There was nothing dull about Lady Brandram, nor about the people who met in her well-appointed rooms, for she possessed a great deal of quiet tact, and was a perfect hostess, in that she made all her guests feel that they were truly welcome, putting them completely at their ease with each other and with herself.

She was a woman with no problem-soul, but one whose chief desire was to appear to advantage at every turn, and to be regarded as the friend of her friends—as in truth she was. Motherly towards all young people, she showed more genuine kind-heartedness to the world in general than childless women are usually capable of.

Since the death of Lord Brandram, some ten years before, she had looked to Sir Hugh Galbraith for that moral support which a woman exacts from some member of the opposite sex, be he husband, brother, or (as in her case) nephew; and more than that, Sir Hugh had largely contributed to the good lady's comfort in life by substantial pecuniary help, the late lamented Lord having been more addicted to the turf than was altogether compatible with providing a proper jointure for his widow. With all his cynicism, Galbraith was a generous man.

Thus it came about that Lady Brandram was enabled to continue her residence in Belgrave-square, and entertain her large circle of friends to her heart's content. To have the rooms filled with well-gowned women and well set-up men was her greatest delight, and to the old lady's credit be it said, she had mastered the secret of true hospitality—to be courteous and kindly to all. Eastern nations understand this far better than we Northerners do; perhaps our manners get frozen up sometimes, or lost in the thick, white fog which so frequently enwraps our British Isles; but it is not altogether the fault of the climate that we are, sometimes, very wanting in *savoir faire.*

On this particular Thursday afternoon, several people were comfortably seated in Lady Brandram's drawing-room. The softly-tinted walls, the rich draperies, and the priceless *bric-a-brac* scattered about, formed a charming background for the dainty toilettes of the women, who had disposed themselves in various lounging-chairs, and forthwith became talkative.

A famous man once remarked that a *posse* of women conversing always reminded him of the epitaph composed for

> "Sophonisba Young,
> Who on the twentieth day of June
> *Began* to hold her tongue."

'Tis true, 'tis pity, and pity 'tis, 'tis true, that men must work and women must talk, or —— but let us draw a veil over the possible consequences.

Across the thickly-carpeted floor the light glowed from numerous shaded lamps, and the scented breath of hot-house flowers filled the air. It was a fad of Lady Brandram's to have the lamps lighted at tea-time, even when the lingering autumn sun forbade their necessity. "It is more cosy," she remarked, "and so much more becoming to the complexion."

Someone, as usual, was talking about the weather.

"One never knows what to put on," sighed Lady Brandram; "yesterday it was hot, to-day it is cold, to-morrow it may be either or both."

"That is true," replied Mr. Comstock; "our English climate is full of unlimited possibilities."

"Life is very flat at present," chimed in Lady Betty; "even Sandown and Goodwood are things of the past, and the world is singing pro tem. to the tune of *tout passe, tout lasse, tout casse!*"

"Not at all, my dear girl," exclaimed Marmaduke Myddleton; "it may be the fag end of the season, I admit, but you need not make out that every thing is verging towards stagnation, just like a teetotum beginning to flap."

"The autumn is generally somewhat depressing," rejoined Lady Brandram, yawning ever so slightly; "with the waning of the social year, London grows more sphinx-like than ever."

"Yes," said Mr. Comstock, "you see a great deal of sorrow all around you, as the winter comes on."

"Oh! I say, old fellow, there is something wrong with you; come and have a drink," said Marmaduke, the last portion of his sentence uttered in an undertone.

"Mr. Comstock smiled. No one ever minded what Marmaduke said, or dreamed of getting angry over his impertinences. "I suppose such ideas strike you as rather abnormal, but when an old fogy like myself lives alone, he does get queer fancies into his head, you know. I like solitude at times, but at my age a man is too apt to regard the shady side of life's pathway as the more frequented one."

"I adore solitude also," said Marmaduke, "but I much prefer it—*a deux.* As to your talk of age, why that is nonsense; you will bobble along for years yet, on the 'sweet shady side of Pall Mall,' too, I'll be bound."

Mr. Comstock paused for a moment, and then said quietly: "I was forty-three last month—nearly double your age, Myddleton—and that is one of those incontrovertible facts which sober a man."

"Why, look at Aunt Mary over there; she is ten years older than that, and as jolly as a sand-boy still."

"Lady Brandram is charming always, and as young as her heart," replied Mr. Comstock with old-fashioned courtesy.

"It seems to me no one is really old now-a-days, when grandmothers are cyclists, and octogenarians figure in the Divorce Courts," said Marmaduke. "But this mud-hole that Lady Betty thinks we are sticking in must get stirred up soon."

"Perhaps the very stagnation you deplore was the author of that new invention, the Modern Woman, with all her train of literature, theories and clubs," said Mr. Comstock.

"Give me the stagnation a thousand times over, bad as it is, rather than that sort of thing," laughed Lady Betty in return. "I sincerely detest the 'revolting' female. Life is vulgar, men and women are often vulgar, but the vulgarity of the New Woman is prodigious."

"She makes men feel like Br'er Rabbit, 'mighty poly,' though I for one do not intend to 'go loungin' roun' an' sufferin'.' Aunt Mary would not like it; she needs me to keep her flagging spirits up," said Marmaduke. "And her spirit flagons down," he added *sotto voce.*

A pitying expression flitted across Lady Betty's face, as with considerable severity in her tone she demanded:

"Why on earth do you call Lady Brandram 'Aunt'? She is no more your aunt than I am."

"That is the very reason, my good girl. I call her Aunt Mary simply because she is not a particle of relation to me."

"What an idiot you are, Marmaduke," laughed the girl in return; "but, oh! my prophetic soul, here is Mrs. Osborne!"

"Beast!" ejaculated Myddleton.

"Marmaduke!" exclaimed Lady Betty in horrified accents.

"She is; I cannot help it."

They had drawn back into a recess partially cut off from the rest of the room by a huge Japanese screen, and were watching the entrance of a lady, of very medium appearance, who bore down upon her hostess with a beaming smile.

"My dearest Lady Brandram, how are you? But I need not ask; I am charmed to see you looking so well; you really seem to grow younger every day. Mr. Comstock too, and to think that I should be so fortunate as to meet you here also"—and the rest of her speech was lost amid the shaking of hands and the clatter of tea-cups.

"Hear that?" demanded Myddleton, from his coigne of vantage. "How I hate, detest, and loathe that female."

" Marmaduke, will you be quiet ? She will hear you."

" No such luck. She always calls me her 'dearest Mr. Myddleton ;' it nearly makes me sick. She is nothing but a—a—a crystallized falsehood !" he exclaimed.

" Well, you need not go near her ; you can leave her alone, surely."

" Just what you cannot do, most innocent maid ; she fastens onto you—positively sticks to you like a sort of social glue."

" Oh ! Marmaduke, what nonsense ! I cannot see why you dislike her so very much. She is always most pleasant to me, though I must say I am by no means fond of her ; she rather rubs me up the wrong way."

" Of course she does. I tell you she is a toad, and therefore poisonous. I have to be polite to her because society demands it, but inwardly I am raving mad whenever she comes near."

Lady Betty laughed. " I certainly never pine for a chat with her, though she is the sort of woman I would not offend for anything. After a visit to her house I always feel a sadder and a sillier girl, but to say that you hate her—that is going too far."

" No, it is not. She is about the most exasperating creature I ever met. Here, Comstock, do not you think Mrs. Osborne is a very trying sort of person ?"

Mr. Comstock, who had strolled away to examine a

beautiful Burne-Jones, which hung on the opposite wall, turned round.

"Trying? Yes, perhaps so. But why do you ask?"

"Why does one do anything in this world? Why take opium or smoke? To gain information, of course, and a precious lot of it you do obtain from your first cigar."

"Will you not have some more tea, Lady Betty?" enquired Mr. Comstock. "Let me get you a cup."

"No, thank you," with an adorable little smile; "I have had two cups already. But, Marmaduke, will not you have some?"

"Me? Oh no! thanks; I do not like tea; it has unpleasant associations for me; tea and frumps, you know, always go together."

"What is that sentiment you are so emphatically expressing?" asked a voice close to him.

Lady Betty and Mr. Comstock started; they had not perceived the approach of Mrs. Osborne, who, cup in hand, stood close behind them.

"I was only remarking," said Marmaduke calmly, in spite of the warning glance from Betty's brown eyes, "that tea and frumps always go together."

"Oh! really," said Mrs. Osborne gushingly; "how very amusing. You are always so witty, Mr. Myddleton."

This speech fell rather flat, for Lady Betty and Marmaduke were silently convulsed—to have opened their lips would have meant eternal disgrace.

"I saw a friend of yours to-day," went on Mrs. Osborne, as no one else broke the silence,—"Sybil Carlisle. Dear girl, she is so devoted to her mother. The old lady is laid up with a bad cold, and Sybil will not leave her to go to the Thornlow's ball to-night. Such a sweet unselfish girl, but rather self-opinionated for one so young—do you not think so ?"

"Evidently, Miss Carlisle has given her a snub," whispered Marmaduke to Lady Betty, who promptly tried to frown him down.

"No, Sybil is clever, and has a great deal of common-sense, but she is not dictatorial," eagerly replied the girl, who was always ready to stand up for the absent ones.

"You think not; ah, well! perhaps you are right, but it is a pity, then, that she should give strangers such a false impression. Someone told me the other day that they thought her so conceited. I assured them she was not, but I fear they did not quite believe me."

"I am not surprised," murmured Marmaduke. "I mean," he continued blandly, "when one has formed an opinion it is sometimes hard to change it."

"Just so," replied Mrs. Osborne, glancing sharply from one face to another in the small group; but childlike innocence was written on all.

"I hear the wedding is postponed again," chimed in Mrs. Quentin, a young and pretty woman somewhat of the *fin-de-siècle* type.

"You do not mean to say so? How very strange! I have often thought that they were not quite suited to each other, not what you might call—very much in love."

"They are awfully in love, indeed they are, Mrs. Osborne," eagerly asserted Lady Betty. "Mr. Desmond just adores Sybil, and she—she is in love with him, too."

Mrs. Osborne smiled the superior smile of the married over the single, and then, for want of further stimulus, the subject dropped. Betty's loving little heart grew very sore at any disparaging allusion to her friend and, knowing well how restless and unsettled Sybil was at that time, she had been deeply distressed over the second postponement of the wedding, for she had made up her mind that, once married to Eric, Sybil would be much happier, with a firm hand to guide her and plenty of love and sunshine to surround her. The vain longing for a public career in which the girl indulged, and the excitability of her finely-strung nature, would calm down and disappear, thought Betty, when the cares and duties of a household fell upon her shoulders. And in the meantime the devoted little friend declined to listen to one word of fault-finding against Sybil.

"I heard the other day that your house in Kensington Square was for sale, Mrs. Osborne," said Mr. Comstock; "is it true?"

"Yes, I am sorry to say it is. We find it too large,

and are going to take up our abode in Inverness Terrace."

"You will naturally feel parting with the old place."

"Undoubtedly. You see it is the house I was born in."

"Specimen of the Georgian period, I have no doubt," put in Marmaduke, serenely.

"Yes, and very well preserved."

This proved too much for Myddleton; a sort of gurgle was plainly audible, though, as he was engaged at the moment in consuming a piece of cake, he presumably only choked. Even Lady Betty and the others could not repress an involuntary smile, for Mrs. Osborne's habit of posing as a young wife, in spite of her forty-five years, was well known. She was a woman with a decidedly middle-aged face, and a preternaturally youthful smile.

A welcome interruption occurred at this moment in the person of Sir Hugh Galbraith, who came in as one sure of a welcome.

"Hugh," exclaimed Lady Betty in delighted accents, "I am so glad you have come back."

"My dear boy," echoed Lady Brandram, "this is a pleasant surprise. When did you arrive?"

"Not two hours ago," he replied, "so you see I have come to pay my respects to you very promptly. Ah! Mrs. Osborne, how do you do? And Comstock, old man, same as ever!"

" We have all missed you so much, Sir Hugh. I am sure dear Lady Betty will be rejoiced to have her companion back again"—this from Mrs. Osborne with a seraphic smile at the girl in question, who, with shining eyes and outstretched hands was welcoming her cousin.

" Thank you, Mrs. Osborne. It is good to be at home again.

" Did you have much sport?" enquired Lady Brandram.

" Excellent, and glorious weather too. The country is grand at this time of the year."

" People have not come back from Scotland yet, and Town is horribly dull," said Lady Betty.

" Yes; even that last resource, politics, is at a discount in September," put in Mr. Comstock.

" Betty," said Sir Hugh, turning to her, " have you seen Eric Desmond lately?"

" He was here yesterday. Why do you want to know?"

" Because I must see him at once on some private business."

" Why did you not come home when he did, Hugh?" she enquired.

" Because I —— could not," he hesitated.

" Would not, you mean," she replied, laughing. " What, or rather who, was the attraction? Come, confess, it was not the fishing that really detained you."

"Nonsense, Betty. Do you suppose I am going to be cross-questioned like this? You should show more deference to your elders."

"And leave the science of 'pumping' to Mrs. Osborne," muttered Marmaduke.

"Sit down, Hugh, and tell me all about your tour, where you went and what you saw," said lady Betty, utterly ignoring the last speaker. She knew it was the only way to shut him up, argument being the joy of his soul.

"All right, little girl," replied Galbraith, with a pleased intonation, (all men like the attentions of a pretty woman) and forthwith they ensconced themselves in the cosy corner, banked by its soft pillows of silk. They were good friends, these two—chums, may be—but nothing more. Brought up in close companionship, they understood one another thoroughly, and enjoyed each other's society, but to Mrs. Osborne, who was surreptitiously watching them, such a state of things appeared simply unintelligible.

She was distinctly one of those narrow-minded people whose circle is a week, and whose starting point is Sunday; a dangerous woman, too, for she was clever in her own way, and contrived to set everyone else by the ears, without getting implicated herself. One does occasionally meet such people in the social jungle through which we all have to travel. They cannot be openly, honestly vindictive like a man, but under a smiling exterior, and with soft words, they sting us, wound us, hurt us, oh! so cruelly. Language is a powerful instrument for the disguising of the truth, and in the mouth of such a woman is a deadly weapon; a hint here, a seemingly careless word dropped there, and lives are wrecked, hearts are broken, faith is shattered. Against such a Society Fiend there is no protection.

CHAPTER XII.

> " He drawsth out the thread of his verbosity,
> Finer than the staple of his argument."
>
> —LOVE'S LABOUR LOST.

IT was late when Sir Hugh rose from the dinner-table that night to join the ladies in the drawing-room. Lady Brandram had insisted that he should remain to dine with her, and with the charming addition of his pretty cousin, the meal had passed off pleasantly enough.

The periodical and lengthy visits of Lady Betty to Belgrave-square had tended to establish the girl more in the position of daughter of the house than that of an ordinary visitor.

Little brown mouse, her aunt often playfully called her, and brown she certainly was, but not very mouse-like. Golden-brown hair, yellow-brown eyes, olive-brown skin, and withal, the tiniest, trimmest, daintiest scrap of humanity in the world—such was Lady Betty. What if she did use slang occasionally, or indulged in small frivolities for her own amusement. Her heart was in the right place, and from the crown of her well-poised head, to the sole of her smartly-shod foot, she was a true gentlewoman.

During the evening she played and sang to her cousin, for whose especial benefit the girl declared she had remained at home from the Thornlow's ball, keeping the egotistical man of the world amused with her merry chatter.

"You do remind me so of one of Ouida's heroes," she laughed, "just as you sit there, leaning back in that big chair, with a slow smile hovering round your mouth."

"How so? Where does the resemblance come in?"

"Just in the *tout ensemble.* She always describes the man, with a capital M, as icily-cynical, and the proud possessor of a tawny moustache, one who has drunk the cup of pleasure to the very dregs."

"And so you think I have drunk of the cup of pleasure to the last drop, eh, little girl?"

"No, not that exactly. At least, I don't know whether you have or not, but you must admit that you have a tawny moustache, and certainly you are very cynical and sarcastic sometimes."

"Only as cynical as life, Betty, after all."

"Why, life is just lovely, 'real elegant' as Miss Almira Pepper said to me the other day. You do not know her, do you? She is a new friend of mine, an American girl, who comes from a place named Eureka—'way out west' she calls it."

"Good gracious! What a name!"

"And she is so amusing, she says I am 'just too cute for anything,'" said Betty, imitating Miss Almira's nasal drawl.

Sir Hugh laughed. "We shall have you talking

like a little Yankee next. How did you come to meet this girl ?"

"She is staying in London with her mother, and they go everywhere. They have heaps of money, and she is so beautiful, and wears such lovely clothes."

"And uses such lovely slang too, I suppose. I am afraid, Betty, you will grow worse than ever now, and be using some terrible American as well as English expressions."

"Pray, why so, Mr. Lecturer ? But, truly, Almira does not say anything very outrageous. Yesterday, her brother, who is just fourteen, did make a funny speech. I had to laugh, it was so comical."

"What did the boy say ?"

"You promise not to be shocked if I tell you ?"

"Honour bright, I promise."

"Well, then, she asked if it was still raining, and he said, 'You bet your variegated socks it am !'"

"Betty !" came in a shocked voice from Lady Brandram, who had been indulging in a surreptitious "forty winks," and just awakened in time to hear the conclusion of the girl's sentence.

"I did not say it, Aunt Mary; it was Almira Pepper's brother."

"You should not repeat such things, my dear; it is not decent; and how do you know whether Hugh wears coloured or black socks ?"

"Aunt Mary," began Betty again, and then stopped. She felt explanation would be useless under the circumstances; and seeing that Galbraith was shaking with laughter, she also gave way to mirth.

It was not until the ladies rose to bid him good-night that Sir Hugh found an opportunity to obtain a private interview with Lady Brandram. At his request she then bade him come up to her *boudoir*, where, undisturbed, he might confide his business to her. The man felt instinctively that in order to gain his aunt's entire collaboration he must first tell her the whole truth; and so, withholding nothing, and in plain, straightforward language, he recounted the events of the last few weeks, laying bare his scheme before her.

Astonished beyond measure, the old lady was utterly dumbfounded, and, throughout the long narrative, sat with bewildered air, as Sir Hugh poured out in eloquent words all the hopes and ideas with which his brain was teeming. When at length he paused, she answered him, as nine out of every ten women in her position would have done, that the thing was impossible, preposterous—and then lightly chaffed him for his quixotism, deeming that after all it was but an idle fancy.

Earnestly he pleaded for her help in carrying out his cherished plans—in fact, for her full participation in his scheme. He showed her that unless she consented to introduce Ursula the whole thing must fall through; and then, in glowing colours, he painted the charms and attractions of the girl, and with consummate tact drew a vivid picture of the reflected glory that would accrue to her as the chaperone of such a beautiful *débutante.* With wonderful power of diction the man strove for victory.

His mind was set on the achievement of this one great object; and as he spoke in low, clear accents, the compelling force within him asserted itself. A faint flush of indecision flickered across his aunt's face. Now and again a nervous movement of the hands betrayed her agitation; but she was an elderly, phlegmatic woman, not an impressionable, unsophisticated girl like Ursula Harlowe, and therefore did not so easily fall under the domination of Sir Hugh's unconsciously exercised power.

Firmly believing that he was using only perfectly legitimate means to induce his aunt to consent to the scheme, Sir Hugh felt a flash of triumph when he saw signs of yielding in her face, and in another moment had drawn her into expressing her views openly. Could he but once get her to write a letter to Mr. Harlowe, begging the farmer to allow Ursula to visit Belgrave-square for a long period, the baronet was sure that the old man would relent, and permit his daughter to come to London.

Now, we all know that they who resort to argument are lost; and so it proved in Lady Brandram's case. After an hour of discussion, and frequent digressions from the subject, Galbraith gathered his forces together in one brilliant summing up. For an instant, Lady Brandram seemed stunned, and there was silence so deep that the sharp tinkling of a small clock in the next room was plainly audible, while Sir Hugh sat forward on the edge of his chair, and bent his eyes upon her face, the muscles of which twitched perceptibly. Something was going thump, thump, thump in her chest—something was slowly tightening around her throat—something was drawing, forcing, driving, compelling her—to what? She might—she must—she would—give way.

It was all over. Then and there Lady Brandram yielded. Unconventionality was rampant, she argued to herself, and if this thing was a trifle more idiosyncratic than her usual actions, what matter? It was nobody else's business, and society at large would benefit by it.

The good lady had not by any means been brought up in the modern roccoco school of behaviour, and found it hard to assimilate the new doctrines of advancement; but, on the other hand, she positively adored Galbraith, and in her eyes he could do no wrong. To please him she would gladly have sacrificed much, but it is extremely doubtful whether in this particular instance she would have succumbed to ordinary influences. Was it possible that for the second time in his life Sir Hugh had conquered through Unconscious Hypnotism?

Thus it came about that, in the dawning, Lady Brandram sat down at her writing-table, and with nervous fingers penned the letter to Mr. Harlowe that was to be Sir Hugh's passport to the old man's consent that Ursula should come to London.

CHAPTER XIII.

"Then came the autumn, all in yellow clad."
—SPENCER.

"A thousand fantasies
Begin to throng into my memory."
—COMUS.

WITH the late fall of the year comes a sense of sadness and of ruth. Something has vanished that will never return again in quite the same guise. Autumn lies brooding over the land, pensive at her own depletion, and teaching us that the joys appertaining to summer are past and gone. The rhythmical sweep and swing of the reaper's sickle is heard no more, and the call of the homing rooks makes the air ring with a desolate sound, while the boisterous wind that comes skirling through the trees causes them to shiver, and completes the ruin by making a clean sweep of the showers of leaves that drop rent and seared from the tall oaks.

It was a sombre day in October, that dull and gloomy month which wears the brown livery of autumn, and the chill white mist was drawn closely across the marshy meadows, like a face-cloth over the features of a dead woman, tenderly enwrapping each distinctive outline, till all are hidden from view. In violent contrast to this depressing scene, the many lights shining through the windows at Deepdene Farm looked cheerful, and while the wind moaned and the rafters creaked, Mr. Harlowe and Sir Hugh Galbraith sat before the big stone hearth, where the fierce, leaping flames darted skyward from the blazing logs, hurling lurid shafts of lihgt against the walls, ere they vanished up the throat of the chimney.

Sir Hugh had lost no time in returning to Arleton after obtaining the letter from his aunt, and as he and the farmer sat smoking in the oak parlour, they discussed, for the second time, the idea that Ursula should leave her home. The minutes passed quickly, for the subject was naturally an absorbing one to both men, and again and again did Sir Hugh reiterate all his arguments in its favor.

"I cannot change my mind. What I told you before still holds good, and I see no reason for making any alteration in the answer I gave you then," said Mr. Harlowe.

"If all my persuasion goes for nothing," replied Sir Hugh, "there is yet one thing which may induce you to reconsider what you have just said. Here," he continued, drawing an envelope out of his pocket, "is a letter from my aunt, to whose care I propose that you should confide Miss Harlowe. Read it. It may convince you, as my words have evidently failed to do, how very advantageous a thing for your daughter this scheme of mine is likely to prove."

"It is not much use, I fear," said Mr. Harlowe, as he slowly opened the envelope, and scanned its contents.

It was a long communication, Lady Brandram having honestly done her utmost to aid her nephew in carrying out his plans.

Sir Hugh watched the reader's face anxiously, but it remained perfectly stolid as the old man's eyes travelled along the closely-written lines, and with a feeling of despair, Galbraith leaned back in his chair, believing that his last effort had failed. It was not his nature to take defeat easily, moreover he had sworn to himself that he would succeed, and to be thus baffled with the goal in view was intolerable.

Silence supervened; then suddenly a low exclamation of mingled astonishment and agitation which broke from Mr. Harlowe's lips caused Sir Hugh to glance quickly at him. The farmer held the last sheet of the letter with shaking hands. Great beads of perspiration stood out on his forehead. Bewilderment, sorrow, and, above all, intense surprise were depicted on his face, as with startled eyes he gazed at Lady Brandram's signature. Galbraith sat dumbly waiting for some explanation. None came, however. With a gigantic effort the farmer resumed his customary demeanor, and folding up the letter, put it quietly into his pocket-book.

Neither of the men spoke for some minutes, and then Mr. Harlowe murmured in a dreamy voice, more as if speaking to himself than addressing his companion: "Twenty years since it all happened, and to-day the chance is placed in my hands to right the wrong which was done them. Can it really be the same woman?" He stopped short, and turning to Sir Hugh spoke in a more normal tone. "You assure me on your word of honour as a gentleman, that this is a genuine offer of Lady Brandram's?"

"Certainly it is."

"And that she is, in truth, your aunt?"

"Yes, my mother and she were sisters. I have spoken of her so often, that you surely cannot doubt my word."

"No, I do not; but you always alluded to her simply as your aunt, and never by name, so that until I read her letter just now, I was totally ignorant of the fact that she and Lady Brandram were one and the same person."

Sir Hugh was puzzled. What was the old man to Lady Brandram, or Lady Brandram to him, that the sight of her name should produce such a marked effect upon him? It was outside the range of all likelihood that they had ever met before, or even heard of one another, and besides, his aunt had not shown the faintest sign of recognition at the mention of Deepdene Farm, or the Harlowes.

"And her maiden name, what was it?" continued Mr. Harlowe.

"Mornington. The family comes from Cumberland. But of what interest can this be to you?"

Mr. Harlowe smiled. "Possibly much. I want to know all particulars about the lady to whom I am going to send Ursula."

Sir Hugh was paralyzed for the instant. Had he heard aright? Had the farmer really changed his mind, and consented? The lights danced before his eyes, and everything looked blood-red in the glow of the crackling flames.

"You will permit Miss Harlowe to go to my aunt then after all, and be introduced into society?" The words came slowly, and scarcely above a whisper.

"Yes, I will allow her to go to Lady Brandram, and be under her care, if—" he paused, and spoke with great earnestness,—"she will swear to treat the girl as one of her own flesh and blood."

"That I can promise you faithfully, but my Aunt shall write you the assurance herself. And I thank you heartily for your belief in me," said Galbraith, rising and offering his hand, which the old man took, and wrung with genuine feeling.

"All right, Sir Hugh. But there is still one person to be consulted; Ursula shall not go unless she really wishes to."

"Where is Miss Harlowe? Can we not lay the scheme before her at once?"

"She is not entirely ignorant of it. I told her a good deal of what you said when you were here last; but at the same time I also told her it was then out of the question."

"Will you speak to her now, or shall I?"

"It is too late to-night. Better leave matters alone until to-morrow, but if you walk over here after breakfast you can then discuss it with her. And now," continued the farmer, "it is twelve o'clock; so I will bid you good-night. I have much to think of, and need a quiet pipe to aid my thoughts."

"Good-night, and a thousand thanks," replied Sir Hugh.

At noon the next day, two figures, a man and a woman, were pacing slowly up and down in the garden, where the golden sun-beams struggled vainly to dry up the sodden ground and make the dripping chrysanthemums hold up their bowed heads.

It had not been a hard task to induce Ursula to favour the new plans, and now Sir Hugh was listening eagerly as she gave a shy consent to his scheme. Her dread of the tremendous change had been gently combatted by his tact and knowledge of the world, but what had really turned the scale in Galbraith's favour was the feeling with which the girl appeared so strongly imbued, namely, that she was perfectly safe when with him. Her implicit trust in the man was wonderful. As she looked up at the baronet, her whole confidence shining in her truthful eyes, Sir Hugh drew back for a moment, man of science as he was, appalled at the thought of all he had taken upon himself. Was it right to tamper with her present mode of life to use her as the expositor of his experiment?

But as they walked to and fro, talking of all the pleasures which the near future held in store, he gradually regained his cool-headedness and tenacity of purpose, and presently the momentary fears which had attacked him were lulled to rest and forgotten.

There is in everyone's life a crisis in the formation of character, which has vast results. Through such a crisis Ursula Harlowe was then passing. Hitherto she had been a child, full of pure, sweet thoughts and simple tastes ; now she was called upon to decide a question which would affect her whole after-life. And each moment, as it flew by, left her more matured, more of a woman.

In her inmost soul the girl knew that she would never have consented to such an upheaval of her present life, if anyone but Sir Hugh Galbraith had been the instigator of the idea ; but as yet she did not try to fathom her motives or feelings any deeper, so that the newly-born secret of her girlish heart was left in the hands of Fate.

Ursula really accepted the proposition for two reasons ; in the first place because she was impelled to do so by Sir Hugh's influence ; and, secondly, because (though she understood it not herself) she loved him and would have followed him to the end of the world. And so another tragedy in the Drama of Life began.

BOOK II.

THE EXPERIMENT IS BEGUN.

"Begun in gladness,
But thereof came in the end despondency and madness."

—WORDSWORTH.

CHAPTER I.

"On with the dance! Let joy be unconfined."
—BYRON.

"Tis the eternal law,
That first in beauty should be first in might."

THE London season had just begun, for it was May, and the six dreary months of winter were a thing of the past, dead like last year's hopes, and now fresh spring flowers covered the earth, and all was fun and frolic.

It was the night of the first great event of the season, namely, a ball given by the Honourable Mrs. Verner. As yet the conservatories were cool, though the dancing-rooms had long ago reached an almost unbearable temperature, and, in the brilliancy of the electric lights, a mad kaleidoscope of colour whirled round and round, in time to the strains of the Hungarian band.

Every one in town worth knowing was there, and the house grew momentarily more crowded. What did that matter? No one thinks that a dance is a real success unless she is nearly squeezed to death, and has her gown torn to ribbands. The hour was fast approaching midnight, and the air felt heavy with the scent of dying flowers, for the decorations were superb. Masses of roses in great china bowls filled up odd corners, bunches of them looked out from among the green wreathing that entwined the balustrade of the broad stair-case, everywhere there were *Maréchal-Niels* and *Gloire-de-Dijons*, pink *La-Frances* and crimson *Jaqueminots.*

Through the series of luxurious rooms, into the dim seclusion of a hot-house beyond, walked a girl with head erect, and the slow, unfaltering step of an old *habituée* of society, and, as she passed the groups of exquisitely gowned women and somewhat *blasé* men, more than one pair of eyes turned to gaze after her retreating form and that of Sir Hugh Galbraith, on whose arm her fingers lightly rested. Very few people had apparently seen her before, and everyone wanted to know who she was and where she came from. As to the men, they of course imagined themselves half in love with her already, having, during the earlier part of the evening, cast many a surreptitious glance at her lovely face and *svelt* figure. The opinions of the women were divided on the subject; some of them genuinely admired her, but the majority were simply curious, and the minority jealous.

On flew the ball, madly, exultingly, regardless of *accroes*, and by supper time the lucky few who had gained an introduction lost no time in informing their less fortunate friends that the new star on the social horizon was Miss Harlowe, a friend and *protegée* of Lady Brandram. Further details about her followed in due course. She was very young, this was her *début* in fact; her relations lived in the south somewhere, very highly connected and wealthy people—and while these and many other statements, more or less true, went from mouth to mouth, the unconscious object of so much comment sought the comparative rest which the conservatories afforded, and there gave herself up to the sad, sweet pleasure of a *tête-à-tête* with Sir Hugh.

"Are you enjoying yourself?" were the first commonplace words which broke the silence between them.

"Intensely," she replied, thinking more of that present moment than of the recent dancing.

"I am glad, but tell me are you satisfied? Does society come up to your expectations?"

Was she satisfied? Ah! Great Heaven! with that gnawing pain at her heart, could she or any other woman ever be satisfied? Resolutely crushing down the feeling, however, she responded gaily:

"The ball is delightful, but as to society, well, you see it is all very new to me yet."

"I forgot, for the moment, that this was your first and only glimpse of dissipation."

"Yes, Lady Brandram never let me go anywhere all through the winter, except to very small affairs. This is my real "coming out" party you know."

"And your first night of triumph," he answered gallantly. "Did I not prophesy your success? And now see, the whole room is at your feet. Lord Kilmainham has been going about raving over your dancing, and old Sir Geoffrey Landon openly declares you will be the belle of the season."

She leaned a little towards her companion, pleased surprise written upon her face.

"How nice of him; he is such a dear old man. But take care, Sir Hugh; too much flattery will turn my head."

"Pretty speeches do no harm when they are true," he answered, "but more wonderful than that you should have won the praise of men, the women, too, have accorded you their share of admiration, and to be clothed in the approbation of the dowagers is to be encased in social armour proof against the darts of the envious. You are success incarnate, Miss Harlowe!" and Galbraith's eyes sparkled with gratified ambition as he spoke, for it seemed to him that on the very threshold of the trial his experiment had achieved an unprecedented result.

It was all quite true. He had not exaggerated the opinion of the fashionable hotch-potch. Ursula was a star courted from her very rising in the social heaven and soon to become largely in the ascendant. Her entrance into society had caused a great sensation. Had not the Duchess of S—— requested that, "the beautiful girl in white with the flower-like face," might be introduced to her? Had not the men one and all fallen down before the dangerously bright glances of her eyes?

"I am afraid you think too much of me," said Ursula timidly.

Sir Hugh was absolutely staring at her, drinking in the perfect picture before him. Suddenly he bent down and kissed her hand. There was no suspicion of familiarity in the movement, it was purely an act of homage to her beauty.

"Forgive me," he said, as she drew back somewhat hastily, and the crimson tide flowed up to her temples and then ebbed, leaving her a trifle pale. "I never knew until this moment how very, very beautiful you are."

The words and tone were chivalrous in the extreme, such as no true woman need have been ashamed to listen to, and yet they stabbed, and then quivered like barbed arrows in that sensitive thing, a girl's fresh heart. To hear speeches of calm, cool admiration (mental admiration one might almost have called it), from this man was agony to Ursula. It was like the touch of unskilled fingers on an open wound.

For the past six months Lady Brandram had endeavoured in every way to fit the girl for her new position in life, and had found her a ready, willing pupil. Ursula's natural instincts were all those of a gentlewoman, therefore, to put on the polish that society demanded was merely a matter of time and association. Her manner, from being shy and retiring, had grown more assured, though still very quiet, and she had also acquired a graceful charm which contact with clever people imparts to an adaptive nature. A real liking had sprung up between the elder lady and her *protégée*, and now on the night of the girl's *début* no prouder chaperone could have been found in all London than Lady Brandram.

Gowned in white satin that hung in severe folds to the ground, and clung to her tall, young figure, as only a Parisian creation can, Ursula had disdained to wear any ornament save a few delicate hyacinths fastened in the laces of her bodice. The gradual passage of months had only served to heighten the girlish loveliness of her face, and that night she looked like a pure, white blossom, amid the display of orchidaceous dresses and *bizarre* fashions which surrounded her.

Lady Brandram had kept the secret of the girl's identity most faithfully. There was not one being in all that vast assemblage who had the faintest suspicion that the beautiful Miss Harlowe was not "one of themselves," a patrician by birth and education; for her ladyship possessed that somewhat rare sense of honour which consists in the ability to keep another's secret. Unless its curiosity is raised by some injudicious remarks, society at large is generally content to accept facts as they are publicly announced, and thus no questioning inflection sounded in the note of praise which was struck in Ursula's favour. She was beautiful, apparently wealthy, and was charming and gracious,—so society adored her, and asked nothing more.

Presently another couple entered the conservatory, where Sir Hugh and his partner were sitting,—two men this time, one of whom was Marmaduke Myddleton, the other Eric Desmond. As they approached, the former said in an excited undertone:

"By Jove! there is the new beauty with Galbraith. Come and I shall introduce you. She is well worth knowing."

"Who is she?" demanded Eric unconcernedly.

"A friend of Lady Brandram's. She has just come out, and is,—but there, you will see for yourself in a moment."

"I am not very keen about new people," said Eric, "and I seem out of touch somehow with the world. Six months of travelling makes a man feel a total stranger on his return to town life."

"Never mind that, you must meet her. As Galbraith's friend you will be sure to see each other often, and by George! she is stunning."

"All right, go ahead then," and in another instant they were standing before Ursula.

"May I introduce Mr. Desmond to you, Miss Harlowe?" said Myddleton, in, for him, unusually formal tones.

Had the whole array of orchids which filled the hothouse suddenly struck him with their tendrils, Eric Desmond could not have been more dumbfounded. No words could express what he felt,—he was absolutely flabbergasted. The name, the face were identical, but,—what did it all mean? How came this girl to be in London, in the heart of an exclusive set? He looked helplessly at Sir Hugh, and caught an expression of supercilióus triumph on the latter's features. What on earth had happened? Somehow or other he managed to bow to her, and then stood dazed and silent, forgetting even to greet his old chum, whom he had not seen since they parted in the little Herefordshire village the autumn before.

"Mr. Desmond and I are not such strangers that we need an introduction," said Ursula, smilingly. "We have met once or twice before to-night, have we not?" with an arch glance at the bewildered man.

"By Jove! You don't say so," said Marmaduke, "but where, and when? It must have been long ago, for Desmond was in America all last winter."

"Yes, it was at Deepdene we met, and——"

"Miss Harlowe," interrupted Sir Hugh, and as it seemed to all present, a trifle hastily, "you must be very kind to Mr. Desmond, he is one of our oldest friends and has been so long away from us that we should give him a hearty welcome home."

"Thanks, Galbraith, old fellow, it is good to know one is not forgotten," said Eric, and so the conversation passed to other topics, and the threatened danger of disclosure was averted. It was seldom that these little *contre-temps* occurred, for Ursula's tact prevented her making any serious blunders, and only once had she narrowly escaped detection. It happened that when talking to Sybil Carlisle, she one day told the girl that she knew Eric Desmond, and on Sybil's enquiring where they had met, the vagueness of Ursula's reply, "Some time ago, in the south of England," had providentially ended the matter.

It was impossible to obtain a proper explanation then, either from Sir Hugh or anyone else, and Eric's equanimity had been too completely overthrown for him to talk to Ursula with any degree of connectedness until he could fathom the present condition of affairs. Some people are capable of behaving and speaking calmly and unconcernedly in spite of all upsetting influences, but to this class Desmond did not belong. Placid and easy-going as he usually appeared, once fairly unhinge him and he was in chaos.

Into this yawning gulf of desultory talk jumped Quintus Curtius, alias Mr. Myddleton. How true it is that Marmadukes will rush in where angels (meaning sensible, every-day folk) fear to tread.

"I do not like talking *en bloc*," he remarked, "please come and have an ice with me, Miss Harlowe. This green-house may be very lovely, but I do not care for plants, and I do care for supper, so let me entreat you to join me in a search of food and fun." So saying he offered his arm with alacrity to the belle of the evening.

Scarcely had they disappeared through the curtained door-way when Eric sternly confronted Sir Hugh.

"What is the meaning of all this?" he questioned, anxiously. "How comes it that Miss Harlowe is here, and in this position?"

Sir Hugh smiled cynically and his lips took a triumphant curl as he replied:

"The world, my dear fellow, is at present engaged in worshipping at the shrine of a new divinity, and I am the originator of the scheme which has given to society its beautiful idol."

Desmond listened as one stunned.

"You brought the girl to London," he said, incredulously.

"Not exactly. She has been for the last six months with Lady Brandram, and has made a brilliant *début* to-night under my Aunt's wing. She is known here as our friend—and Eric, I must ask you to keep the secret of her parentage inviolate."

"I cannot make head or tail of this business," he answered. "For Heaven's sake, man, give me some explanation of it?"

And Sir Hugh did. Knowing that Desmond had it in his power to spoil everything by making injudicious disclosures regarding Ursula's antecedents, Galbraith felt that the only way to secure his friend's silence was to be perfectly frank with him and then appeal to his honour to keep what had been said strictly private. As briefly as possible the baronet gave him an outline of the scheme and its development, and then proceeded to enlarge on its success.

"Why did you not tell me of your intention to do this thing, when we were in Arleton?" asked Desmond, interrupting the flow of his friend's rhapsodies.

"Because, my dear fellow, the idea was then only in an embryo state, and you went off so unexpectedly to America that I had not time to enlighten you later on the subject."

"You might have hinted to me about it before I left."

"Impossible. Matters were only finally arranged in October, and when I returned the second time from Deepdene I learned that you had left two days previously for New York on some urgent business."

"Yes, it was a serious inconvenience having to go away then. For one thing it necessitated the further postponement of my marriage, and also it completely upset all my plans for the winter's work."

A sudden influx of people from the ball-room checked further confidences. Several men joined them, and the conversation drifted to other topics, foremost amongst which was an openly expressed admiration of the new beauty.

Eric Desmond walked away. He was too preoccupied with what he had heard to care to talk with anyone just then; he wanted to be alone for a few minutes in order to try and place his thoughts. He had listened attentively to all Sir Hugh had said, and was now trying to see his way clear to keeping the secret, and anxiously revolving in his mind the great question of right and wrong in the matter. To foist such a gigantic deception on society was in itself a crime, so he argued, and his strict code of morals forbade him to hearken to the voice of sophistry which whispered that the end might justify the means.

The end—what would the end be? The girl would probably become in truth one of the "upper ten," capable of holding her position, and growing day by day further removed from her old status. But when she was securely established in her false tenure—what would happen then? Marriage, most likely, with a man far above her in station, and marriage with a man who was ignorant of her origin. This was an anti-climax to be avoided at all hazards. The thing could not, must not, go on. Galbraith was mad to have entered upon such a foolish scheme. Experiment be hanged! Could Sir Hugh not see the sin of experimenting with flesh and blood for his own selfish psychological ends? The girl was a good girl, and it was cruel to raise her to a position which was untenable; to fill her with spurious hopes and vain ambitions, all of which could only lead to a grand finale of disaster. That Lady Brandram should have countenanced the deception surprised Eric hugely, but then women were incomprehensible creatures he averred, and not to be judged by a man's ordinary standard. Right was right and wrong was wrong in his eyes, and here was a clear case of folly which he felt it his duty to oppose ; so the result of his ruminations was a firm determination to prevent the continuance of Sir Hugh Galbraith's experiment.

CHAPTER II.

> "Thought is deeper than all speech;
> Feeling deeper than all thought;
> Souls to souls can never teach
> What unto themselves was taught."
>
> —CRANCH.

"HERE you are, dear," said a soft voice beside him; "I have been wondering why you did not come for our last dance," and Sybil Carlisle looked reproachfully up into the stern, purposeful face of Eric Desmond.

"My darling, I am so sorry; but I have been worried about something, and I fear forgot all else in my annoyance."

"Come and talk to me now, as an atonement; I have hardly had a word with you since your return yesterday, and we have such tremendous arrears to make up," she said, drawing closer to him.

"Letters do not count for much, do they, sweetheart?"

"No, one cannot write half one would like to say."

"I have just been introduced to Miss Harlowe. Now, there is something you could have written to me, Sybil. Why did you never tell me about her? You might have known that I should be interested in hearing of anyone who was a friend of Lady Brandram."

"I did mention her to you several times, Eric. Do you not remember I told you that she had come to stay in Belgrave-square and how much I liked her."

"Was it Miss Harlowe you referred to when you spoke of a girl called Ursula?"

"Yes, of course, that is her name."

"Ah!—I see now. I did not connect the two before."

"You knew her long ago, then? I think I remember that she told me once she had met you somewhere in the south. Do you like her, Eric?"

"Yes, I do," he replied, but his tone belied the words somehow. It was distinctly unfriendly. The news he had recently heard from Sir Hugh had made him unreasonably irritated with Ursula.

"She is beautiful, and everyone is raving about her to-night."

"She certainly is lovely," and this time his tone was more cordial; for what will not a woman's beauty accomplish, even to the softening of such a stern moralist as Eric Desmond.

"Do you admire her very much?" enquired the girl anxiously. After all, this man was her lover, and all true women are a little jealous by nature.

"No one in their sane senses could help owning the fact of Miss Harlowe's unusual personality; she is simply superb."

Now it happened that at this moment Ursula and Marmaduke strolled by quite close to where Eric and his *fiancée* were sitting, and, with a man's customary faculty for blundering, Desmond remained silent, gazing at the *débutante*, and apparently totally oblivious of everyone else.

"Eric," said Sybil quickly, "why are you looking so queerly at Ursula Harlowe?"

"Do not be fanciful, dear," he replied with a smile; "surely a man can look at a pretty girl without being accused of doing anything peculiar."

"Oh! yes, of course, but you looked just now as if you had some special interest in her."

"What nonsense, darling; I have no special interest in any woman but you," and the love-light shone for an instant in the tender look he bent upon the girl at his side.

Marmaduke meantime had been exerting himself to an unusual extent in order to entertain his partner. Conscious that he was the cynosure of many envious eyes, he stalked through the ball-room filled with a pardonable sense of vanity at being the cavalier of the much-sought-after beauty, and, presently, when Lady Betty and Mr. Comstock joined them, the chatter of tongues flowed apace.

"It is a fact, I assure you, the supper-room was so hot that the jelly had not enough strength of mind to stand up in its dish, but drooped in melancholy floppiness all over everything," remarked Marmaduke, airily.

"How very nasty," laughed Lady Betty Mornington.

"Beastly sticky, I called it," said Myddleton.

"Marmaduke, I fear your language leaves much to be desired."

"But not much to the imagination," said Mr. Comstock.

"No, for unlike the 'sheeted dead,' you not only 'squeak and gibber in the streets,' but for the matter of that, in the house as well."

"Oh! come I say, do not be so rough on a fellow. Miss Harlowe, I appeal to you, would you really wish me to cultivate silence?"

"There are so many kinds of silence, which one do you mean?"

"Well, you see, I never heard of more than one—the great and awe-inspiring silence of stupidity."

"How about the silence of wisdom?" asked Mr. Comstock.

"Merely a synonymous term for that of an owl, and really to cultivate owlishness would be a trifle beyond me," said Marmaduke defiantly.

"You must not forget that kind of silence which tells far more than the truth it pretends to hide," put in Lady Betty.

"What do you mean Betty?" enquired Ursula with a puzzled look.

"Oh!" lightly tapping her fan against her lips, "I refer to the silence of hints."

Ursula did not look as if this explanation had conveyed any definite enlightenment to her mind.

"By Jove! talking of silence, I wish to Heaven that Mrs. Osborne would cultivate it a little," said Marmaduke. "She button-holed me in Bond Street this morning, and talked and talked till my head fairly reeled."

Everyone laughed. Mrs. Osborne's playful habit of way laying people, and squeezing all the gossip she possibly could out of them, in order to repeat it to the next friend she met (with many frills tacked on, of course) was well-known amongst the set in which she moved.

"What, or rather whom, do you discuss?" said Sir Hugh, who had joined the group just in time to catch Marmaduke's last remark.

"Do not ask me; I could not tell you. Really that woman's loquaciousness should be punishable by law. After half an hour of it I escaped, feeling like a bloated anaconda; her conversation is positively the stodgiest thing I have ever had to digest."

"Whilst yours is light and airy in the extreme, eh, my boy!" laughed Comstock.

"At any rate it would be inadvisable to let the fresh air of truth blow in on some of her speeches," said Sir Hugh sarcastically.

"Why? Do you think it might give her a bad cold?" interrupted Lady Betty.

"Yes, a regular moral chill, by Jove!" replied Marmaduke. "But I say, Galbraith, why do you not tackle her yourself someday? I would give a fortune to hear you pouring out a bucketful of cynicism over her bubbling balderdash."

"Please do not use such frightful expressions, Marmaduke," said Lady Betty. It sounds just like a young crow learning to caw, and the effect is awful."

"If I were to do as Myddleton proposes," said Sir Hugh, "I should feel that the question might fairly be raised as to which of us was the common fool."

"Your words would probably carry weight, though, Galbraith," put in Comstock.

"More so than her dress to-night," murmured Marmaduke, as if apostrophizing the orchids. "It at any rate has very little weight with her, for it consists only of—"

"Marmaduke," interrupted Lady Betty sternly, "you ought to be sent home; you are not fit to remain in decent society."

"My dear girl, I did not make her gown, and if one of the straps gave way, and it—well, it slipped a little —it was really not my fault."

"Marmaduke, will you be quiet? You really are irrepressible."

"How often must I assure you that I did not have anything to do with it. It was just one of those things which happened," he protested.

Laughing, and with gay words, the others scattered off in different directions, leaving Lady Betty and Marmaduke for the moment *tête-à-tête*.

"Give me this dance, Betty, will you?" he requested humbly.

"You always tread on my toes, and walk over my gown," she demurred.

"What does that matter, as long as you are enjoying yourself? But, seriously, I promise not to offend in that line if you will dance this one waltz with me."

"Very well. As you say, what does it matter if one goes home in tatters, as long as one has a good time."

"And that you always have. No scent of the wall-flower about you." And with such light badinage they passed on into the ball-room and joined the throng of revolving couples.

Amongst the dancers were Ursula and Sir Hugh. It was not the first time they had been together that night, but it was their first waltz, and as his arm slid gently round her supple waist and her hand was firmly clasped in his strong fingers she felt the old, strange thrill of something more perfect than aught else in life steal through her veins. Throwing her head far back the girl looked into his face, gazing deep down into those abysmal eyes. In an instant she was once again completely under the control of his Unconscious Hypnotic power.

They were waltzing. Her breath came quickly, her heart beat to suffocation, and then throbbed into quietude, as a violin throbs at the touch of a master-hand, and dies away in a low wail. She was not herself—for the moment she was his—her love, her life, her very soul were all in his keeping. On they floated through the multitude of dancers and the pungent scent of crushed roses, the hum of the band sweeping them forward, dreamily, languidly, as a river flows slowly down to the sea. The violins grew louder, then lower—one could hear the caress in their tones—and still they drifted on, and on, and she knew that she loved this man with a love passing sweet, fairer than Heaven more fatal than Hell.

Suddenly the music ceased, and the silence fell on her heart like lead. As the last minor chord of the waltz died away, and the last smooth, swaying glide of that strange dance brought her to a stand-still near an open window half-screened by palms, Sir Hugh's hold over her snapped suddenly like a taut string, and with a sigh of awakening she realized that the dance was over.

With palpitating breath the girl leaned against the window-frame for support, partly shielded from the glare of the ball-room by a thick curtain, and struggling fiercely for her lost self-control placed one hand on the sill of the sash thrown open to admit the cool night air. Little she guessed that as she rested there, too blinded by the dazzling lights to discern any object outside in the dingy London square, a man, a veritable ghost out of the past, was standing within three feet of her trembling figure, and with scowling face and muttered curses was glowering at Sir Hugh Galbraith, who bent solicitously over her, fanning her hot cheeks with a white feather fan.

CHAPTER III.

> "I shall go my ways, tread out my measure,
> Fill the days of my daily breath
> With fugitive things not good to treasure,
> Do as the world doth, say as it saith."

DURING the six months which had elapsed between the day when Ursula first came to London to be the guest of Galbraith's aunt and that eventful night in the following May when she made her eminently satisfactory *début*, many changes had taken place.

A great friendship had sprung up between her and Lady Betty, for there was something in the steadfast character of the farmer's daughter which attracted and commanded the respect of the frivolous little butterfly, whilst, on the other hand, Lady Betty's goodheartedness and irresponsible gaiety rapidly won the affection of the more sedate girl who had never before cared for the companionship of those of her own age.

Intimacy both with Lady Betty and Sybil Carlisle had been an excellent thing for Ursula, for from them the country maid picked up many little ideas and ways which, trivial in themselves, all helped her to hold her own in the presence of society, and at the same time free girlish intercourse with two such friends served to give balance to her character, which hitherto had run to the extremes of utter childishness and preternatural maturity.

Day by day Lady Brandram grew more attached to the sweet-natured girl, and finally ended by taking Ursula entirely into her warm, capacious heart. Gradually the sense of the unfitness of things died out in the elder woman's mind, and, as her *protégée* became accustomed to the smaller details of fashionable life and quickly adopted the superficial ways of society, she almost forgot the existence of that Rubicon which divided them.

Sir Hugh had settled down in his old chambers, and spent much of his time frequenting scientific meetings and lectures, attended an occasional ball or dinner party, and never for one moment lost sight of his goal. Week after week he watched the development of Ursula's character under the new condition of things. Often he would talk to her, and, possessing the happy faculty of drawing out what was best in others, would lead her on to tell him many of her thoughts and ideas, so that through this medium he was able to ascertain what effect the transplantation was having upon the girl's peculiarly unsullied nature.

To Galbraith she was still only the embodiment of his experiment. He had the strength of purpose to carry out his plans consistently, but that sweetness which is sometimes stored up in the hearts of strong men was, certainly, lacking in him. Had the man been less engrossed in the psychological side of the question he must undoubtedly have felt the influence of her beauty and loveliness, but as it was, he seemed to be totally blind to the woman—all he saw was the subject.

His platonic flirtation with Lady Betty had rippled on through many phases; but, intermittent as it was, and distinctly of the cayenne pepper type, it yet very often had the power to hurt Ursula. Jealousy means love, and love means jealousy; and as it was only too true that the girl had slowly, surely, but at length completely, given her whole unfrittered affection to Sir Hugh, she could not help noting and disliking the cavalierlike attentions he paid to his cousin and Lady Betty's matter-of-fact acceptance of the same. The very coolness of the girl's reception of his trifling courtesies irritated Ursula. To tell the truth, she did not quite know what she wanted. She hated to see Lady Betty take matters so easily, and yet had the latter shown any signs of warmer feeling for her cousin she would have been even more deeply wounded.

People in love are always unreasonable. They do not like their idols to be disparaged, and yet they will quarrel with anyone who dares to adore them too much. This fluctuating feeling of jealousy did not however, seriously interrupt the even tenor of the friendship which existed between the two girls—one of them was too well-bred, and the other too thorougly sweet-natured for that—and probably no one was more totally innocent of any intention to wound than little Lady Betty herself. Sir Hugh was her cousin, and therefore partially her property, and as she never saw any token of the grim tragedy going on at her feet, she naturally enough flirted and frolicked with him to her heart's content, never caring a jot for consequences nor bothering her pretty head over possible contingencies.

A girl who, unasked and unsought, gives her love to one of the opposite sex, is commonly called unmaidenly; and well indeed she may be if she allows him to see that she is, metaphorically speaking, on her knees before him, ready to ask for his affection in return for that which she has bestowed upon him of her own free will. To allow a man to guess her secret—to permit him to know that he possesses her devotion before he has shown in an unmistakable way that he desires and returns it—is simply to make herself despicable in his eyes and to forfeit all her girlish self-respect; but in Ursula's case it was different, because never for one instant did Sir Hugh imagine that she entertained the smallest particle of affection for him. She adored him passionately, but of this he knew nothing—her secret was all her own. Not once, by word or look, had she ever betrayed the love which filled her heart.

What a strange thing love is after all! It can no more be controlled than the restless waves of the sea—it comes from who knows where, or how, or why? So love is not at the command of ourselves; it is a thing given to us, placed in our souls, and is as eradicable as the very germ of existence—sweeter than life—stronger than death. So it had come to Ursula

Harlowe. At first she did not understand. It had crept into her heart unawares, and shown itself in a hundred little ways, in a desire to be with the man she loved and to please him. Each time they met it grew stronger, and each time his innate force dominated her she fell more deeply into the toils. How far this love of hers was the result of the extraordinary influence he exercised over her, or how far his great power over her personality was the consequence of her love for him, it was impossible to determine; but taken together, they formed a chain of iron, binding her body and soul to the man who was tampering with what he was totally ignorant of.

For many years Sir Hugh had studied occult science, and probably as the result of being so steeped in mysticism he had become endued with a great deal of latent personal magnetism. Yet it could not exactly be said that he had either magnetized or hypnotized Ursula into falling in love with him. For that would be to accuse him of wilfully exercising an unlawful power over the girl, whereas he was totally innocent of using any conscious force. But the fact remained that each time his curious power mastered her she became more one with him, and as she believed, loved him more deeply. Who could say where love ended, and hypnotism began? Whatever was the cause of its great strength and deep sweetness, whether it sprang from undue influence or not, the love of Ursula Harlowe for Sir Hugh Galbraith was in itself pure and womanly, such a love as a man might be proud to possess and a woman proud to bestow.

On her return home after Mrs. Verner's ball, Ursula having bidden Lady Brandram an affectionate good-night, and dismissed her maid, wrapped a warm dressing-gown around her and sat down before the fire to think. With wide sad eyes she gazed into the living coals, as if she would fain read her future in their glowing depths. She had been very much upset after that last waltz with Sir Hugh ; never before had the girl felt his influence so keenly, and even yet her nerves and brain were throbbing with an answering emotion, just as the strings of a delicate instrument will quiver and vibrate long after the master-hand has ceased to play upon them. Often before when Galbraith's power had controlled her volition she would instinctively obey his slightest wish, or carry out faithfully any trifling suggestion he might make, and thus the habit grew strong upon her to submit herself entirely to him ; she thought as he thought, formed her opinions on his, and in all things acted as his will influenced her to do—she was in his hands like a piece of thread without a knot at the end of it ; he could draw her through any crisis, guide her through any combination of circumstances.

That night her heart was aching with the weight of its burden of love. "Is it always so," she murmured to herself, her tired tears dropping wearily, "that a man whom a woman loves will not love her? Must this go on all my life?" She was so worn out with inward struggle that the sobs came faster, as she thought of the daily fight to conceal the truth from Sir Hugh. Life was one long piece of acting. When in his presence she must guard her eyes, her tongue, her very thoughts—must feign indifference, friendship—anything rather than that he should see one tiny glow of the love-fire which burned so fiercely within her.

It was a hard task to act, act, act, till she began to wonder whether the loving unloved girl, or the cool, indifferent woman, was her real self. In public the mask must ever be on. Poor little Ursula! The very pure-souled nature which made her so susceptible to Sir Hugh's powerful influence was her salvation now. In her creed, to have allowed him to see that she loved him unasked would have meant something beyond compare. No! he must never, never learn the extent of her folly, she would go on acting in public and loving him in secret, playing her part in the tragedy of the world, but as long as she lived he should remain ignorant of the truth. Verily the path of folly is sometimes as clearly defined as the path of reason.

So Ursula wept on. But a woman who can shed tears has not come to the worst stage yet, and presently she roused herself and, with the inherent buoyancy of youth, began to think of the other side of the picture—of all the triumphs that kind fate had showered upon her that night, and of the sweeter, brighter aspect of her love.

It made her heart very tender to turn from the thought of the things which might have been to the thought of the things that were. After all there was something very comforting, very soothing, in that love—it was all hers—and she had given it to him, her friend, for he was that at any rate. It did not hurt him that she, a little country girl, loved him. To pour out the wealth of her soul at his feet, to worship him in secret, to obey him, to please him, to pray for him, that was all she lived for.

Oh! you blind philosophers who tell us of the degeneration of love and of its short duration—you little know how full of beautiful, true love the world is. It is often so well hidden that your mundane eyes cannot see it, but it exists nevertheless, bright as a Heaven-born thing, a feeling such as angels know and only devils dare to mock at.

Sir Hugh Galbraith was not a fool, nor more blind than his sex, but so carefully had Ursula half-consciously guarded her secret that he was as ignorant of her feelings towards him as an utter stranger might have been; and it must be recorded in his defence that had he realized the extent of his unconscious influence over her, or even known that it existed, he would have abandoned his scheme entirely rather than play on the susceptible nature of a young girl. He saw, of course, very plainly, that she was quite *en rapport* with him, that he could bend her inclinations and thoughts to his own, but this he put down solely to his superior knowledge of the world, and the commonly accepted fact that a simple, untaught mind will generally follow the lead of a vigourous masterful example. Of his damning, damnable power he knew nothing, and so on rolled the course of events, and one poor little soul was caught up, and whirled into the maelstrom of love, semi-hypnotized, and wholly pathetic, to be flung breathless on the shores of lethal sweetness, which means the Death of Hope.

CHAPTER IV.

> "With curious art the brain, too finely wrought,
> Preys on itself, and is destroyed by thought."
>
> —CHURCHILL.

> "Snapping a solemn creed with solemn sneer."
>
> —BYRON.

IT was very pleasant to step out into the soft morning twilight, after the heat and crowd of the ballroom, at least so Sir Hugh Galbraith thought as he and Eric Desmond sauntered leisurely down the flight of stone steps that led from Mrs. Verner's hospitable front door, and stood for a moment on the flagged pavement below, to light their cigars before entering a hansom.

Glancing over his shoulder as he threw away a burnt-out-fusee, Eric noticed that an ill-dressed man had stopped close behind them, and was watching Sir Hugh intently, with an evil expression on his face. "Poor devil," thought Desmond, "one of the homeless race no doubt," and without further comment dismissed the circumstance from his mind. But presently, while Galbraith was directing the driver to take them to Upper Brooke Street, to the house of David Comstock, Eric's attention was again attracted to him, for with clenched fist upraised the man stood glaring at the baronet, with a hellish vindictiveness emblazoned on every feature, and the light from a street lamp falling full upon his face, his form clearly outlined against the dark background of the houses. Desmond thought the loafer looked more like some diabolical apparition than a being of human flesh and blood.

"Do you know that man? Quick, look, there he goes," exclaimed Eric sharply, as the vehicle rattled off over the cobblestones.

"Who? Where? What do you mean? I do not see any one," replied Galbraith.

"Ah! he is out of sight now. It was a man on the roadway, who was staring in your direction as if he wanted to annihilate you."

"Bah! Nonsense! The champagne has gone to your head, old man. Imagination runs races with your thoughts, and evidently runs to win." Sir Hugh laughed nonchalantly; he was too utterly drenched with success to pay any heed to irrelevant subjects.

"Believe it or not as you like, I tell you I saw him as plain as a pike-staff, and more than that, I have seen his face before somewhere."

"Possibly, though truth to tell I am somewhat incredulous as to the existence of this man with the murderous expression. But then we are all skeptical now-a-days; it is the temper of the times, the *zeitgeist* is eminently so."

"Like the flowers that bloom in the spring, that has nothing to do with the case, and for Heaven's sake, man, give us no cheap cynicism to-night."

"Your temper seems slightly out of joint," retorted Galbraith.

"You are right; I am thoroughly upset." Then after an almost imperceptible, pause Desmond went on, "I want to talk with you seriously, Hugh. Will you listen to me fairly and squarely?"

"Go on; I know what you are going to say, and it is of no use, but I will listen if you like," and the baronet settled himself back into the cushioned corner of the hansom, and waited for what was to come.

"Give up this experiment as you call it. No good can come of it, and you are only storing up unlimited misery both for yourself and Miss Harlowe;" and as he spoke, in his earnestness Eric laid a firm hand upon his companion's arm.

"You are far too pragmatical. Can you imagine for one moment that I shall abandon a scheme which has already, at its very commencement, attained such a vast success?"

"But think of the other side of the question. Think of the girl, young,—beautiful,—unprotected. What sort of future are you preparing for her?"

"A glorious one! A triumphal march of conquests and admiration!"

"That is altogether too vague. What substantial benefits can ever accrue to her from this senseless pageantry?"

"It is not vague, only I suppose I omit to make it clear, or possibly the fault lies with your own understanding."

"You seem to regard this girl merely as a specimen, and are so intent on watching the progress of her development that you forget, or else are regardless of the suffering you will inevitably bring upon her."

"You called my cynicism cheap a few moments ago, but now you are guilty of cheaper sentiment."

"Cheap or not I mean every word of it. I do not believe there is one touch of humaneness in your whole being, or you would give up your diabolical experiment. Galbraith, I appeal to you, relinquish this matter, and send her back—home to her father and her friends, who are her equals. You are trying to solve a social problem which has never been fully stated, the difference between what is and what ought to be, and believe me, you can never really succeed. You are so cold by nature that you do not realize what a horrible sin you are committing, whilst I, by the light of the love I bear for the one woman which the world holds for me, can see the pitfalls you are preparing for Ursula Harlowe. Give it all up, Hugh, and remember how a greater than you or I once said, that 'the Ideal is after all only mental, intellectual, conceived, while the real alone is true and genuine.'"

"You are right, in so far as that the foundation of all things must be real and true; but the further development must equally be brain-evolved. No, Desmond; for the last time I refuse to—By Jove! here we are, so there is an end to all argument."

Most unwillingly did Eric pause in the discussion, but events as trivial in themselves as the stopping of a hansom at its destination will often checkmate the strongest of us.

No. 63 Upper Brooke Street was very like its owner, old-fashioned, squarely built, and of goodly proportions, albeit the crimson-striped awnings, and window-boxes massed with flowering plants, loaned to the place an air of modernity. Mr. Comstock had lived there for many years; in fact, ever since that memorable day when a sudden rise in Spanish consols had brought to him fortune and a prominent place on the Stock Exchange. He was a man of middle age, commonplace and somewhat prosy, but with a big heart. That night, in accordance with their promise, Sir Hugh Galbraith and Eric Desmond had dropped in to have a smoke with him after the ball.

As they drew their chairs around the fire, which in the chill of a May dawning was by no means unwelcome, a feeling of *bon camuraderie* led Comstock to open his lips and pour forth an unusual flow of language. The sum and substance of it all was the new beauty, Miss Harlowe. But one-sided conversation palls after a time, and soon he fell to asking questions of the other two smokers who, according to their respective fashions, parried the direct attack. Sir Hugh told him that he knew just as much about the *débutante* as the geologists know of what they are pleased to call the "glacial period," which was simply nothing at all; and Eric Desmond, like all right-minded men when they get nonplussed, grew angry, and puffed away at his cigar in moody silence, refusing to vouchsafe more than an occasional monosyllabic response.

It was plain that the grizzled, unromantic David Comstock was very much struck by Ursula's loveliness. He had known her for some months, and had often enjoyed the pleasure of her society at Lady Brandram's house; but that night the flame of love had been lighted for the first time in his lonely old heart.

Eric saw that the man was really *épris*, and this fact only served to heighten his resentment against Sir Hugh, for was not the very complication he most dreaded already looming up in the distance? When they were once more in the street, and pursuing their way in the direction of Galbraith's chambers, Desmond again gave vent to his wrath. A quarrel appeared imminent. On the one hand was a man of fixed, ideal purpose, and on the other one of stern determination. What could come of it but a fracas? In the lowered voices people affect when deeply in earnest, they went all over the old ground, thrust and parry, parry and thrust, until Eric brought matters to a climax by saying, with an abominable assumption of dogmatism:

"Your arguments admitted (though, remember, I

deny their validity), you are throwing Miss Harlowe into the society of men she may dance with, talk with, flirt with, but—can never marry."

Sir Hugh stopped short in his leisurely pace, and replied:

"Can never marry whom?"

"She cannot marry a gentleman," said Eric sternly, and as if he were hammering in a long nail.

"Why not?"

"Good Heavens! man, because she is—she is—"

"A pure, good girl, and a fit wife for any man."

"But a daughter of the people all the same. How could she marry anyone who was ignorant of her origin?"

"My dear fellow, you talk as if Miss Harlowe were of the very scum of the earth. I have not taken her from the shambles of sin, poverty and unspeakable wretchedness, nor yet from that world which only begins to live after midnight. She is at the present moment in every respect your equal and mine, consecrated to higher ends than a vegetable life, and fit to wed with any man of our acquaintance."

"I am not accusing you of flagrant imbecilities, but of those errors to which abstractionists of your kind are liable. But to be bold is not to be brave; and if you impose on the credulity of society with this fraud, so unhinged and unhinging—your audaciously enacted scheme and a vast calamity will inevitably go hand in hand."

"Say what you please, croak away like any other bird of ill omen, but I tell you again that Ursula Harlowe may marry the highest in the land and yet confer a favour on him. Bah! Marriage does not cancel every other obligation, and for a man to set himself up as an amateur St. Simon Stylites is ridiculous."

"You know very well, Hugh, that where the wife is beneath the husband in birth, both, as a rule, will sink to the bottom of the social Dead Sea. A clever woman may sometimes succeed in pulling up a man to her level, a man can pull up a woman—*never*. Softly but cruelly he is dropped, and she—"

"Cheap sentiment again, and bad at that," sneered Sir Hugh. "Whatever I am totally ignorant of I declare to be the result of profound study, but you blazen your want of knowledge far and wide. For the sake of your reputation for sanity, go, my dear Eric, and live in a cave or, like Rousseau, on a tree-top, and thereby spare the world your vacuous diatribes."

"Hugh, Hugh, do not gibe so bitterly. There is little enough faith left in the world, God knows."

"Am I not evincing ideal faith, in this very matter?"

"No, you are willfully poisoning it in this girl. Sooner or later she will waken to the reality of her position, and in that moment her faith in you and mankind will die, and with weary feet she will travel across the great desert of unfaith stretched out between her and her God."

Desmond walked on, heedless that with the increasing speed of his stride he was gradually leaving Galbraith in the rear. At that moment the sharp report of a pistol rang out clear and sudden, close behind him, cutting through the moist air of dawn. Turning instantly Eric saw Sir Hugh reel forward and come crashing down upon the pavement, his face striking the curb with a sickening thud, as when flesh is dashed against a hard substance. So convulsive was the shock of this occurrence to Desmond's mind, checking as it did a mighty rush of thoughts, that the impulse to retrace his steps and raise the prostrate man was purely mechanical, a triumph of inculcated philanthropy rather than a voluntary action. As he bent over Sir Hugh, and then looked around for assistance, he saw, not ten yards off, the same evil-looking creature who had attracted his notice on leaving Mrs. Verner's house, standing with ghastly face and staring eyes, a smoking revolver in his right hand. Eric started forward as if to seize him, whereupon the man uttered a harsh laugh, and, flinging the weapon into the road, ejaculated the single word "avenged," and sped away into the shadows of a cross-street.

Scarcely a few seconds had elapsed before a motley crew of people and policemen were surging around the two men. Crowds gather quickly in London, even at the early hour of five o'clock in the morning.

Sir Hugh's face was literally smashed in on one side,

and the blood came slowly drip, drip, drip, onto Eric's coat, as he supported the baronet's head. Mercifully unconscious of all that was going on, Galbraith lay quite still as his friend deftly bound a handkerchief round his bruised features. Desmond lifted him into a passing cab, and drove, with all possible speed, to the wounded man's chambers.

So they took him home and laid him on his bed, and a great surgeon came and dressed his wounds, and looked very solemn; but when the doctor finally said: "It is all right; he will live," Eric's heart gave a great bound, and his "Thank God" was a *Te Deum* and *Benedicite* rolled into one.

Once during the hours of insensibility that followed there was a gleam of recognition in the sick man's eyes, and he murmured, "Promise—to—keep—it." And Eric replied, "I promise to keep your secret for the present." Thus in the end did the heart rule the head of the man of sense, and Fate fought on the side of Sir Hugh Galbraith and won another victory.

CHAPTER V.

"A spirit in my dreams
Hath led me to thee."

EXTENSIVE search was made for the would-be murderer, but all in vain.

It appeared that just before the shot was fired, Galbraith, hearing footsteps, had turned to see who was following behind him, and that simultaneously with his recognition of Tom Scott came the sharp ping of a bullet, and he knew nothing further until he awakened to consciousness, in his own room. Of the identity of the man who first dogged his steps and then tried to murder him that night, Sir Hugh did not entertain the smallest doubt; he had in the flash of time before he fell, clearly recognized the features of Ursula Harlowe's ill-favoured lover, and in all probability he owed his life to his sudden movement; for either that, or else bad aim on his attacker's part, had caused the shot to glance round his ribs without striking any vital organ, or inflicting more serious injuries than great loss of blood and a nasty wound.

A few days later Galbraith lay in bed with the windows thrown wide open, in order to let the soft spring air have free access to every corner of his room, and the heavy smell of a number of hyacinths, blooming on the table, came to him in whiffs, as the breeze blew now stronger, now fainter, across their white and purple bells.

"Any fresh news, Eric ?" enquired the baronet, as his friend came in about three o'clock in the afternoon.

"I am sorry, old boy, but there is not, and even the detectives are now giving up hope. Everything is being done that it is possible to do, but the scoundrel must have got clear away out of the country, or else be cleverly hidden in one of the slums."

Sir Hugh lay silent, turning the matter slowly over in his mind.

"It is a strange thing," he said at length. "I cannot understand why Tom Scott should have attacked me in that manner. The man must have a bee in his bonnet, or else be harping still upon that old string of ridiculous jealousy."

"There is little doubt to my mind but that he followed you to London, and tracked you out, with the deliberate intention of doing you an injury."

"The thing is absurd; I had no hand in Miss Harlowe's refusal of him. There must be some deeper motive than that to account for such a demonstration of hate."

"It is hard to form any conclusion," replied Eric, gravely; "there may be wheels within wheels of which we know nothing."

"I am not altogether disappointed that the affair has come to a deadlock," said Galbraith meditatively, "and can hardly tell whether I really do wish the man to be caught."

" You fear that if he were brought to trial Miss Harlowe's name might be dragged into the case ? "

" Exactly, and that I would avoid at all hazards."

" I quite appreciate your feelings there. I saw her to-day ; she and Lady Betty were shopping in Regent Street this morning."

" My aunt tells me that Betty is most anxious to come and see me, but the doctor says, 'no excitement and no visitors.' So the dear little girl sends me flowers every day instead, and more messages than would fill a volume."

" How soon do you think you will be able to get up ?"

" Goodness knows ! They tell me I shall not be all right again for three weeks."

" By the bye, Lady Brandram met me on my way here, and told me to tell you that she would look in about six o'clock to see if you wanted anything."

" Thanks. Clarke, however, is really a splendid nurse."

" I see you have got the bandages off your face to-day. That plaster is a great improvement."

" Yes," replied the baronet, with a feeble attempt at a smile, " it is certainly prettier, and much more comfortable ; but my cheek was so mushed up on that beastly curb-stone that it will take some time to regain its former shape."

The door opened softly, and a man entered with the noiseless tread of a well-trained valet."

" Beg pardon, Mr. Desmond, but the doctor's orders were that Sir Hugh was not to talk long, sir. It is four o'clock, and I have got his medicine here."

" All right, Clarke. I'll be off now, Hugh, and give you a chance to rest. Good bye, old man, till to-morrow," So saying, Eric rose and, with a cheerful nod, left the apartment. He had been very casual in his allusions to Ursula when talking with Galbraith, knowing that the latter must on no account be excited; but he had neither forgotten nor condoned the existing state of affairs.

After Desmond had gone downstairs, Clarke proceeded to close the windows and pull down the shades, so that only a subdued light shone into the room.

" Perhaps you will take a sleep, Sir Hugh ? "

" I may. Do not disturb me until Lady Brandram comes. She will be here at six o'clock."

" Very well, Sir Hugh."

" And, Clarke, have the fire lighted at once ; it gets cold about this time."

" Yes, Sir Hugh."

Soon a ruddy glow, and the pleasant sensation of warmth that pervaded the atmosphere, lulled the sick man into a quiescent state. He was alone in his great, luxurious room, the blinds drawn down, the doors shut, no sound to disturb him, no brightness to distract him—everything was conducive to slumber. Gradually drowsiness fell upon him, his thoughts grew confused, vague, and seemed on the point of submergence—when, vivid as a lightning flash, a vision rose before him.

Like the crack of doom a name struck his ear—"Ursula." So blinding was the mental picture of the girl that he pressed his finger-tips tightly against his eye-lids to shut out some of its intensity. Like a radiant vision from the world of unexpressed beings, she swayed and swerved before his dilated pupils; then the luminosity of her face faded slowly and the undulating movement of her figure stiffened into rigidity. With this cessation of motion on her part, his reeling brain grew steadier, and he noted that she was very pale.

Then, as touch by touch the vision grew more blurred and indistinct, Sir Hugh strained every nerve to see clearly the features of Ursula Harlowe. Only to keep her—that was his one desire. To keep her—to keep her—to keep her—Ah!—she was going—she must come back! "Ursula—Ursula—Ursula," he cried, each word ringing out in a low, vibrant tone of command and entreaty.

She was gone. A chill breath touched his forehead—he heeded it not—all he felt was Ursula—all he thought or wished or imagined was—Ursula.

The minutes passed, the coals fell with a splurge in the grate, a few flames leaped up and quivered into smoke, and the daylight grew less, and the firelight warmer. Yes, it was warm—very warm—Sir Hugh could scarcely breathe. A queer smell surrounded him—it must be those hyacinths—there were too many of them. He remembered vaguely having heard some one say that in great quantities they were poisonous, —and so heavy—so suffocating. But Ursula liked them. No, it was the eider-down quilt that was so oppressive on his chest—it was nearly choking him. She might have taken it away with her—he did not want it. Oh! those hyacinths! That sweet, sickly perfume! Why did she not destroy them?

It seemed as if two warring elements within the man were struggling for the mastery over him—one that calm power of self-control which was the main characteristic of his nature, and the other an involuntary force stronger than he was. The more he fought for the mastery the more did that strange sensation overpower him, as he lay there convulsed and with heaving limbs.

"Ursula!" Where was she? He wanted her. "Ursula! Ursula! Ursula!"

Ah! the door was opening, she was coming back to him—his beautiful vision—the culmination of his experiment. Yes, but not as she had looked half an hour before. Now she was all in black, and her face so white. The vision was not as perfect as it had been, but all the same it was—Ursula. With a desperate effort he raised himself on his elbow and gazed at her. Merciful Heaven! how pale she was—perhaps she was dead, and this was her spirit come to bid him an eternal farewell!

How straight she stood there in her trailing black garments, her hands falling limply at her sides, her eyes so wide open that they looked like shining disks!

"Ursula!" The name broke from Sir Hugh's lips with an involuntary spasm of over-wroughtness.

"No answer,—only a slight parting of the pale lips —just a tremor through the rigid frame.

"Ursula," and again Galbraith felt suffocating, a dim fear of the girl, so sharply outlined in black and white, coming upon him.

Was she going to speak? Her lips trembled. Her eyes stared at him with great, distended pupils as before.

"I have come, Hugh."

An awful horror crept through his veins, his heart almost ceased to beat, the numbness of terror froze his limbs as ten thousand fiendish, blaspheming voices shrieked and gibed at him. His reason was going, —ah!—he was mad—mad—mad! That vision was no longer a vision to him. It was Ursula Harlowe in the flesh.

A sane man was lying upon his bed, raised into a semi-elevated position by means of one supporting elbow, and looking fixedly at the figure of a girl standing in the middle of his room. The moment she had spoken, Galbraith had experienced a severe mental shock. He understood that it was the real Ursula Harlowe who stood there, so ghastly and immovable, confronting him with an inexplicable reproach. And the force that was strangling him died—and he saw things as they were.

Though usually composed to a degree which irritated all his friends, the sudden appearance of the vision, followed by that of the girl herself, had totally unnerved the baronet. To span with thought the circumstances before him, was but the work of a moment. She was either insane, or else in a drugged state. What could be done in order to induce her to go away ? Clarke was liable to come in at any instant, and Sir Hugh dreaded to think of the consequences that might ensue should anyone learn of her visit to his chambers alone, and at such an hour.

" Miss Harlowe," he said, in a firm voice, " You must not stay here. I beg of you to return home at once."

The girl took absolutely no notice of his words, but continued to stand there, her great, luminous eyes fixed upon his.

He spoke again, this time more determinately.

" You must go home at once, Miss Harlowe."

Her face expressed a slight touch of wonderment.

" Why do you send me away ? " she said mechanically. " I came because you called me, Hugh. I heard your voice so plainly saying, ' Ursula, Ursula, Ursula !' "

" This is absurd. Do you not see that it is inadvisable you should visit me here ? Some one might come in, and then ——."

" What would that matter ? You needed me, and I came. That is all."

Galbraith was now nearly beside himself with anxiety. He must induce the girl to leave the room before she was discovered. A very agony of sweat broke out upon his forehead as he thought of what might come to pass if this mad escapade ever reached the ears of the world, so harsh in its dicta, and so censorious in its judgments. Yet there she stood, utterly indifferent to his urgent request. What should he do? He could not call for assistance—that would be to publish the matter at once—and to move from the bed in his present weak condition was an utter impossibility.

He glanced at the clock; it was nearly six. In a few minutes Lady Brandram would be there, and then—. He grew desperate.

Suddenly it flashed across his mind that she must be walking in her sleep. He would try stronger measures.

"Ursula Harlowe, go home at once, I command you," he said, with all the force he could summon to his aid.

Not one iota did this dictatorial speech move her.

Sir Hugh was fast becoming exhausted, for his strength, but feeble as yet, could not sustain the great demand he had made upon it during the last half-hour.

Tick, tick, tick, went the clock on the mantel-piece. It was five minutes to six. Now or never must he save the girl. With excruciating pain the baronet raised himself to a sitting posture, and, gazing sternly into her eyes, said:

"Go home."

Instantly she took a step forward, and then steadily, but oh! so slowly, moved toward the door, which on her entrance she had left ajar.

Hush! What was that sound? Great Heaven! It was Lady Brandram's voice—she was coming along the hall—talking to Clarke. Galbraith's head swam, and stars danced and reeled before his eyes in a blood-red tarantella. Foot-steps were coming nearer; he grew sick with the continued strain of suspense. Ursula had almost reached the doorway on the inner side, but it was all over—he could not save her now. In another moment his aunt would enter the room, and then all would be lost.

But where was the girl going? She had turned aside and was now walking rapidly towards the farthest corner of the room. Was it Providence that caused Ursula to make her exit, not by the usual way, but by a smaller door which led into an unused room, and thence out onto the main staircase of the building?

She was gone, and Sir Hugh fell back on his pillow, and gasped for breath. He felt faint and weak, and the relaxation of his muscles was fraught with almost as much pain as relief. For a few moments the man lay there, oblivious to every sensation save that of rest in mind and body, but as things came slowly back to their normal condition he began to wonder why Lady Brandram did not enter the room. He listened and heard her still talking to Clarke in the passage some yards away from his door. Everything was quite safe then; Ursula must by this time be well on her homeward way; and so he fell to wondering why and how the girl had come to his chambers, for it was altogether a most unprecedented affair, and quite inexplicable to him, unless, as he ultimately supposed, she was a somnambulist.

But then, how on earth could she be walking in her sleep in the dusk of a spring afternoon? As he pondered on these things, carefully revolving the situation in his mind, and unable to come to any reasonable conjecture on the matter, his eye, as it wandered restlessly from one object to another in the room, fell on a splash of white lying upon the floor, in conspicuous contrast to the dark colours of the Turkey rug. With the fretful fancy of an invalid, he stared at it, wondered what it was, and "why the deuce, has Clarke left it there." Just then the fire blazed up, and in the brighter light he recognized it to be a pocket handkerchief. And there was lace on it—he could see that clearly now. A pause. Why, it must be Ursula's, of course—and, if so, her name must be on it, and he could return it to her some day—women had such an absurd habit of having their names embroidered on everything—there would be no difficulty in identifying it. Then too—but his aunt—she was just coming in—she would also see it, and, probably, recognize it—no, that must not be, for how could he account to her for its presence there? She was far too keen-witted an old lady to be bamboozled with any trumpery excuses.

What should he do? At all risks he must gain possession of that damning little piece of evidence before Lady Brandram entered the room. But how to do so, that was the question. There was nothing for it but to reach it himself. Could he manage this?

With a violent effort Sir Hugh slid both feet onto the floor. The upright position made his head swim, but he could not afford to lose any time in waiting. So, steadying himself by means of the chairs and tables, the man commenced a toilsome journey across the room. Stumbling, staggering, he reached the little, white, tell-tale bit of cambric. Hark! his aunt's step at the door, a gentle knock, and a voice, saying: "May I come in, Hugh?" Where could he hide the thing? Ah! He was falling. With an almost superhuman wrench Galbraith flung the handkerchief into the glowing coals of the fire, and came crashing down like a broken tree, while the blood soaked in crimson patches through the bandage wound around his wounded side.

Thus Lady Brandram found him, but she never learned why, or how he got there, nor could anybody else get a reasonable explanation from him on the subject. His lips were sealed by honour, so no one ever knew that a man of the nineteenth century had done an act worthy of the chivalry of the middle ages ; and at what might have been the expense of his own life, had saved the name of a girl from the breath of undeserved gossip.

CHAPTER VI.

> "Of all the passions which possess the soul,
> None so disturbs vain mortal's minds
> As vain ambition."
>
> —EARL OF STERLINE

SIR Hugh Galbraith was very ill. As the result of his mad exertions, fever had set in to an alarming degree, which was not to be wondered at, such an act as he had compassed being under the circumstances little short of suicide. Many days elapsed before the man recovered the ground he had thus lost.

Ursula Harlowe had been in a very chaotic state of mind ever since the date of the baronet's relapse, though exactly what was the matter with her, or why she seemed so completely out of gear, the girl herself could not have explained. She distinctly remembered having gone upstairs to her own room on that afternoon, taking with her "*Marcella,*" and having there settled herself into a big cosy chair near the window, to enjoy a quiet read. That she had perused over fifty pages of the book was certain, for a recollection of their contents remained quite fresh in her memory on the following day. But Ursula imagined that after reading she must have fallen asleep, for it was nearly dark when consciousness returned to her, and the room felt very cold. With a sudden impulse, she tried to rise, but the effort proved painful; her head ached, and a curious tiredness numbed every limb, just as if her nervine force were temporarily paralysed. She was far too cold, however, to sit still any longer, so, with a violent spasmodic jerk, she finally got up, and walked over to the dressing-table. She fumbled in the dim light for a match-box, which she eventually found, and then proceeded to light a candle.

The ghostly flame flickered in her eyes, and the looking-glass reflected back a face white as death and totally expressionless. As, with dragging steps, Ursula again crossed the room to ring the bell, she noticed several footmarks distinctly visible upon the delicate grey ground of the carpet, and stooping to examine them, she saw that they were wet. She then glanced at her feet. Her boots and her skirts were muddy too. What did this mean?

With a curious haste she tore off her dress, unlaced her boots and threw them with an unreasoning disgust far out of sight under the bed. Then she tried to think, but nothing came of it; she was mentally in chaos.

That evening Lady Brandram, noticing how pale and weary the girl looked, questioned her closely; but Ursula merely replied that she had been reading all the afternoon, and had thereby given herself a bad headache. That she felt ill and very tired, she was fain to admit; but a sensitive fear of ridicule sealed her lips with regard to those muddy garments in which she had found herself, and for which she could in no way account. The more she thought about them, the more bewildered she grew, and also became dimly conscious that it was a subject best kept secret—something to be vaguely ashamed of.

When at the conclusion of dinner they entered the drawing-room, the elder lady said, kindly:

"Sit in that big chair by the fire, my dear, and do not try to do anything but rest for the remainder of the evening. It will never do for you to be ill now, when poor Hugh is so much worse."

Lady Brandram had told the girl of the baronet's relapse.

"You must indeed be anxious about him," replied Ursula, for was not she herself sick with pent-up agony on his account? "But I hope it may only prove to be a temporary attack, and that he will be really better to-morrow."

"I trust so, I trust so, but he is very ill to-night. How pale you look, child!" for Ursula had suddenly whitened to the lips. "Why, you are chilled to the bone!" as she took one of the girl's hands in hers Suddenly the old lady uttered a sharp exclamation.

"What is it, dear Lady Brandram, what is the matter?"

"Nothing child, only an old woman's fancy."

Ursula looked up curiously. The elder woman was gazing at her in mingled sorrow and astonishment. She had stroked back the rippling masses of the girl's bronze-red hair, thus drawing it severely away from her temples.

"There certainly is a resemblance," she went on. "Do you know you are very like a sister I once had, my dear. Several times before I have fancied I could trace it, but now, with your face so pale, and your hair pulled back just as she used to wear it, you remind me more than ever of my sister Isobel." And Lady Brandram sighed heavily.

"Did you love her so much, and is she dead?" enquired Ursula half-timidly.

"Yes, dead and at peace many years ago. Hers was a sad life, and one full of disasters, most of them the outcome of her own willfulness, and some of them dealt to her by the stern hand of Providence. When you are gay, child, the likeness to Isobel flies, but when you look as you do to-night, wan and white, with your eyes full of unshed tears—just so, with your hair gathered back—then I seem to see my sissister once again, as she looked in the days long gone by."

Ursula sat very still, listening to these reminiscences of a past that had nothing in common with hers, and wondering in a tired way if the real history of this Isobel's life had been as full of sadness as her own. She felt very nervous and exhausted, and the gentle touch of Lady Brandram's hand soothed the irritation of her brain.

The days that followed were dreadful ones to Ursula. Mingled with her anxiety about Galbraith, who for twenty-four hours had lain between life and death, there ran an undercurrent of puzzlement at the strangeness of her experiences on awakening from that supposed sleep. During this time she derived great comfort from her friendship with the Carlisles, for Lady Brandram being kept in constant attendance on the invalid, the girl would have passed many solitary hours, if it had not been for Sybil.

Mrs. Carlisle and her daughter lived in a very quiet neighbourhood, though their tiny house was situated at no great distance from the more fashionable quarters of London. Thus the girls met nearly every day, and grew through constant association to take a genuine interest in each other's affairs.

Since Eric Desmond's return from America, nothing definite had been arranged in regard to his wedding. He had come home full of the hope that Sybil would at once and forever renounce her aspirations after public fame and be content to marry and settle down quietly, as his wife; but before many days had elapsed he perceived that the old fever was still strong upon her, though he noted to her credit that she strove hard to crush it down to a certain extent. It was a great pity that two people who really loved each other very deeply indeed should be thus wrenched apart by means of their strongest sentiments.

Eric was a man of most dogmatic principles and, even at the sacrifice of all he held dear on earth, would not give way in this particular instance; whilst Sybil, aglow with the fire of enthusiasm, and having been brought up in easy-going laxity, taught to regard art as supreme and publicity as quite compatible with respectability, could not at all understand his idea that art was for artists of the Bohemian world alone, and that a public career destroyed all the sweetness and all the womanliness in a girl's nature, rendering her totally unfit for the daily avocations of life.

One afternoon the glorious spring sunshine was flooding all the world with brightness, and nature, warmed by its friendly glances, burst into a grand revelry of life, sending forth myriads of tiny buds to celebrate the season of awakening. Ursula was seated in Mrs. Carlisle's pretty drawing room, her furs thrown aside, and a rosy colour staining her cheeks. Sybil lay back in a low basket-chair, her hands clasped idly in her lap, whilst her mother sat placidly knitting, an occupation in which the old lady indulged at all times and in all places.

"I wish you had been there last night to hear him, Ursula," said Sybil. "I can never tell you how beautiful it was. You have to hear the man himself play, to understand what the perfection of his touch is."

"You enjoyed the concert, then?"

"Enjoyed it? I should think so. All the music was good, but Sarasarte was like one inspired. His rendering of the 'D Minor' was magnificent."

"It must be a wonderful thing to make music which can hold the attention of hundreds of people," chimed in Mrs. Carlisle.

Sybil bent forward. "It is the most enthralling sensation one can know. To feel that you and your violin together are making sounds sweet as an angel's song, that the harmonies are floating upward in a surging mass, now crashing with the excess of power, now trembling like stars just lost in the light of day, —softly caressing as they fade away in a low kiss of pain,—sobbing as if fraught with all mortal woe—Oh! it is glorious; nothing on earth can equal it," and the girl's features quivered as she spoke thus ecstatically of her beloved art.

So engrossed were the three occupants of the room, that Eric had opened the door and stood on the threshold unperceived. Only when Sybil ceased speaking did he come forward to greet them all with his usual slow courtesy.

The girl sprang up, and flushed uneasily; she hated to be caught rhapsodizing by her *fiancé*, for the simple reason that she knew how he looked down on all such conversation and called it rubbish, so she commenced hastily to turn the talk into other channels. But Eric was in no humour to be led hither and thither, either conversationally or otherwise; he was in a distinctly aggressive mood and was feeling very over-done. Now, when a man is tired, and just a wee bit out of temper besides, he will invariably rake up some old grievance, and wave it defiantly in his companion's face; not because he has any particular reason for so doing, but merely because he wants to have a good grumble.

With an abrupt jerk, Desmond interrupted Sybil's flow of commonplace remarks by saying:

"What were you talking about when I came in just now?"

"Sarasarte," replied the girl briefly.

"He did play well last night. I have never enjoyed a concert more," admitted her lover. "But then it is his vocation," he added with a touch of superiority.

"If I could play as he does, I should ask for nothing more on earth," said Sybil.

"But you do play beautifully, dear; what further do you want?" rejoined Eric. "There is no one to whom I would so gladly listen. In private," he added.

"Now please do not start the old discussion. No good ever comes of it and, besides, it would not be very entertaining for Ursula," replied Sybil, who felt in no humour to travel over debatable ground.

Her friend smiled. She had heard the question worried out before.

"Miss Harlowe agrees with my opinions, I think," said Desmond, "so I should have an ally on the subject for, like me, I am sure she prefers the quiet pools to the mad mill-race of life. Do you not?" turning to Ursula.

"For myself, yes. But then I am not clever like Sybil."

"Oh! now you are hedging."

"Not at all. For me there i nothing but to lead a peaceful existence. I am only one of the mediocre kind. But Sybil is different; she might become famous if given the opportunity."

"There I differ from you. Notoriety she might acquire—fame never."

"Eric!" indignantly protested his *fiancée.*

"I mean no slight to your music, dearest; but only in her home and in the society of her friends can a true woman shine. Fame is only for the very few, and 'stars,' unless of the first magnitude, are simply gazed at, criticised and admired by a host of sycophants in their own world, who are eager to share the spurious greatness of the clay idols which they themselves have set up. Immortal fame is rarely achieved even by genius."

"If you are going to talk platitudes, I give in," said Sybil impatiently, "but I cannot see why you should wish to condemn me to live always at the dead level of dullness. No, mother, I did not mean that exactly," she continued, as Mrs. Carlisle looked up in surprise, "but you know how I long to go on the stage, to make a name for myself with my violin, and it seems so hard—"

"Can you not be satisfied with the admiration of those who know and love you,—of your friends and acquaintances?" interrupted her mother gently.

"No, I cannot, and that is the truth," replied the girl.

Eric looked annoyed, and Ursula heartily wished herself somewhere else. The atmosphere was growing oppressive.

"You know my wishes, Sybil. There is no use in giving the conversation a personal turn," said Desmond quietly.

"Everything seems tangled up," replied the girl wearily. "I want to do one thing, and you want me to do another, so that I am forever being pulled in one direction or dragged off in another."

"Our life does seem rather a story of knots at present, little girl."

"I think any one might envy and try to copy such great artists as Sarasarte, Paderewski or Paganini," said Ursula, by way of helping out her friend.

"Those you mention are all men, Miss Harlowe," said Desmond.

"True art is sexless," put in Sybil quickly.

"Now, do not argue any more,—there is a good girl," said Eric persuasively.

"Well, I will not if you will promise not to be so aggravating," she replied.

Desmond laughed. His temper had regained its customary sunniness, and he plunged forthwith into a general dissertation on the ground work of true genius.

The three women listened with varying degrees of attention. Ursula did not understand all he said, and was, moreover, torn in two on such occasions by her staunch championship of Sybil, and her secret feeling that Eric's arguments tallied with her own convictions.

"Materialism may be *fin-de-siècle*," said Sybil, interrupting a long, carefully-worded sentence of Desmond's, "but it is not art."

"What a formidable antagonist you are; you never miss a chance to retaliate," he said, smiling.

"Girls are, evidently, more collected creatures than you imagine. You constantly talk of the genius of men, but remember the old fences of prejudice have been thrown down, and the professions, science and, above all, art, are now open to women of capable minds."

"In the nineteenth century, intellect appears to be king," said Mrs. Carlisle.

"Yes," replied Eric, "and it is brain against brain in the daily battle."

"Unless for once we take the bit in our teeth, and bolt, leaving all behind us," remarked Sybil, triumphantly.

"You never can count on what a woman will do next," rejoined her *fiancè*. "They are often more exaggerative than artistic. Look at the modern stage."

"Some artists, of course, follow a wrong path," assented Sybil, impartially, "but dramatic intensity governed by talent is superb."

"Yes, when enacted by a past-master," replied Eric.

" Or mistress," interpolated Sybil.

" Women, when they go on the stage, so often act in a rudderless fashion, and forget the subtle distinction between power and hysteria," said Desmond.

" I know whom you are thinking of," murmured Sybil, quizzically.

" Whom ?" inquired her lover, looking nevertheless rather caught.

" My great admiration, Mrs. Patrick Campbell."

Desmond laughed, but did not deny the accusation.

" I like to see an artist who carries you away with her and makes you feel that what she is acting is a reality," continued Sybil.

"That can be done in two ways: by genuine dramatic strength, and by an excited rendering of anti-climaxes."

"There are many actresses in London who are graceful, refined, even delicate in their art," said Ursula.

" That is true, and all honour to them for it; but actresses and artists are of their own world, beings set apart from our every-day life, and as such to be admired or condemned."

" Your views are bounded by old traditions, Eric," said Mrs. Carlisle.

" And where should we be without traditions ?" he rejoined earnestly. " Why, they are the basis of all artistic work as well as the main props of life."

Presently Sybil drew Ursula aside into the bay-window, for the purpose of exchanging a few words in private with her friend, whilst Eric and Mrs. Carlisle continued to keep up a desultory conversation.

"There you see how it is, Ursula," the girl said tempestuously. "He lays down the law and expects me to give in entirely."

"Never mind, Sybil. It is only in this one thing, and even if he appears dictatorial, never let him see that you find him so. Be true to yourself, dear."

"I love him very deeply, and that is why his opposition on this point, so near to my heart, hurts me extremely and destroys a little of the romance of our engagement." Sybil looked both sad and perplexed.

"All the same be brave and face it boldly. Make the best of things with that sweet grace you know so well how to use."

"But how can I help protesting against such wholesale dictation, such a crushing of all my day-dreams and hopes?"

"Then give them up. Surely, for his sake you could do much."

"Yes," assented Sybil, doubtfully, "but that would mean giving up all."

CHAPTER VII.

"Give me good proofs of what you have alleged."
—CROWN.

"MY dear Sir Hugh, why do you not marry your aunt's charming young friend, Miss Harlowe?"

Had the ceiling come down upon his devoted head with a thundering crash, the young man to whom these words were addressed could not have been more utterly taken aback.

"It takes two to make a bargain, Mrs. Osborne, and perhaps Miss Harlowe may have other projects in view," he replied, with studied deliberation.

"Just as if you could not make any girl fall in love with you if you wanted to." This was said in her most effective manner.

"Really, Mrs. Osborne, you overrate my capabilities. Miss Harlowe is a charming but very sensible girl, and is the rightful guardian of her own heart."

"But then, my dearest Sir Hugh, it would be such a delightful match. You have wealth and position; she has beauty—at least so many think, though I have heard several aver that she is a trifle—just a trifle—*bourgeoise*," with a swift glance at the baronet.

"Indeed," replied Galbraith coldly.

"By the way, you know her so well, doubtless you can tell me who her relations are."

"Most delightful people, I assure you."

"Yes, but who are they, and what part of England do they come from?" with persistent curiosity.

"They are friends of mine, and live in one of the Midland counties," replied Sir Hugh nonchalantly.

"And their name?" eagerly.

"Harlowe, of course," with a quiet smile.

"Oh!" was Mrs. Osborne's only rejoinder.

She was baffled, and saw plainly that it would be very difficult to get any further information out of Galbraith. Nevertheless, she continued:

"But tell me who she is, dear Sir Hugh? People do not drop from the clouds, as it were."

"Oh! ah! I thought I had already told you. Miss Harlowe is the daughter of Mr. John Harlowe."

"Yes, but surely you know something more about her than that."

"I am a sadly ignorant man, I fear. But I can tell you this much, also: Miss Harlowe is extremely beautiful."

"Of course; but then one likes to know whom one is talking to, however charming and lovely they may be."

"As I have just remarked, she is the daughter of Mr. Harlowe, of Herefordshire. More than that I do not know."

"I never heard of the family. There are Harlowes in the south. Very good people?" interrogatively.

"Are there?"

"Yes. Have you ever met them?"

"No, never."

A pause. Then Mrs. Osborne started on another tack.

"A number of men seem to admire the girl very much. Perhaps one of them may prove lucky enough to win her for his wife. Mr. Comstock, for instance, seems quite *épris* in that quarter."

This was said more by way of drawing out Sir Hugh than for any other definite purpose; but, not deeming that it required an answer, he remained silent, and Mrs. Osborne, perceiving with her quick eyes that the suggestion did not in the least disturb the young man's serenity, concluded that he really was not particularly interested in Ursula.

She had called on Lady Brandram that afternoon with the express purpose of finding out something about the girl of whom everyone was talking, and on learning that the mistress of the house was "not at home" had almost forced her way into the drawing-room in order to (as she explained it) "pay a visit to poor, dear Sir Hugh." The latter was now fast recovering from his accident, and had at his aunt's urgent request come to stay in Belgrave-square.

He was lying on the sofa. A soft light from the rose-shaded windows flooded the room, and there was nothing to break the silence save the monotonous tick, tick, of a small ormulo clock.

Into this soothing atmosphere came Mrs. Osborne,

bringing with her a draught of malicious amiability, and instantly Sir Hugh was on the defensive. She was so curious about other people's affairs, so meddlesome, and yet so sweet withal, that her conversation reminded him of nothing so much as a chocolate cream. And then, too, her talent for conversational embroidery was enormous, and the perpetual occupation of her leisure hours.

At present her mind was running persistently on one topic, namely: "Who was Ursula Harlowe?" Now, when Mrs. Osborne laid herself out to discover anything, no power in heaven or earth, no amount of snubbing or coldness, could balk her. With an evergreen smile and a kittenish manner, she questioned and insinuated, until by sheer bluff or point-blank attack she had gained the coveted knowledge.

That some mystery was attached to the sudden appearance of the new beauty in London society she felt convinced, even more so since her chat with Sir Hugh, who she saw was determined to avoid all direct answers to her questions.

The baronet meantime had not been having a very happy half-hour. He knew his visitor's little ways of old, and steeled himself to bear much; but when he perceived that she was playing a deeper game than usual, and that the fabric of his scheme was threatened from such an unexpected quarter, he summoned all his wits to circumvent her and was by turns cynical and caustic. But Mrs. Osborne was far too pachydermatous a person to pay any attention to such trifles.

One little fact especially attracted her notice during the conversation, namely; that though Sir Hugh very calmly regarded the idea of any other man marrying Ursula, he winced perceptibly every time she alluded to the possibility that he himself might fall in love with the girl. With quick intuition she felt certain that some secret reason underlay the dislike he evinced to having his name coupled with that of Miss Harlowe. And she was right, for much as Galbraith had vaunted that Ursula was fit to wed with any man in London, the notion of making her his own wife came to him in very different guise. Such a thought was preposterous, and made him shrink as from something that jarred upon his more refined sensibilities.

"I must really say good-bye now, dear Sir Hugh," chirrupped Mrs. Osborne. "I promised Mrs. Quentin not to be late at her garden party, and I see it is already four o'clock."

"You have some distance to go," he remarked politely.

"Yes, it is not an unpleasant journey though, at this season of the year. I shall, of course, see Lady Betty there. Any messages?"

"My love. Between cousins, you know, that is always allowable," he replied.

"Oh! quite. Only," archly, "there are cousins — and cousins. Good-bye," and with a beaming smile Mrs. Osborne vanished.

Sir Hugh closed his eyes. Peace fell again upon the room. "I have given her a Roland for her Oliver this time," he muttered. "Confound the fiendish little busy-body! She may do more harm yet with her prying tendencies."

The baronet had felt a little awkward on his first meeting with Ursula the day he arrived in Belgrave-square, for he had not seen her since that awful afternoon when he lay ill and she had come to him so strangely; but her complete unconsciousness of any untoward circumstances helped to put him speedily at his ease. For his own part he entertained not the smallest doubt that the girl was a somnambulist.

At first he was undecided whether or not to inform Lady Brandram of what had happened, but on reflection determined to keep silence, for, as he justly argued, how could he tell his aunt the story without implicating the girl in a most unpleasant manner?

To be thus thrown into daily companionship with the man she loved so passionately in secret, tried Ursula not a little, yet at the same time, the present, in which he had so large a share, was very sweet to her.

When Mrs. Osborne reached Blackheath, she found a vast crowd of well-dressed people wandering up and down Mrs. Quentin's grounds, which looked fresh and green in their new spring garb. One of the first persons Mrs. Osborne saw was Lady Betty.

"My sweetest girl, how charming you look this

afternoon. I have just left Sir Hugh Galbraith, with whom I have had such a delightful chat. He sent his love to you," with a simper, "and so many messages. All the while I was there, the dear fellow positively could do nothing but rave about Miss Harlowe. Ah! I see her over there," gazing at Ursula through her tortoise-shell lorgnette. "He seems to admire tall girls immensely."

"That is meant for a dig at me," thought Betty, but she only said:

"Is it not nice that he is so much better?" and sipped her tea in a meditative way.

A low-church curate of the croquet-playing order here claimed her attention, and Mrs. Osborne moved away in search of pastures new. Presently she met Mr. Comstock, upon whom she beamed effusively, and to whom she told three untruths in four minutes. The kind-hearted man endured martyrdom heroically for a while, but was wandering off into the land of his own thoughts when Mrs. Osborne brought him up with a jerk.

"You must promise me not to repeat it, but they say Sir Hugh is going to marry Miss Harlowe."

"What?" gasped Comstock.

"Hush, do not speak so loud. It is not announced yet, but everyone thinks it will be a match, and really I begin to believe it myself. This afternoon he has done nothing but rave to me about her."

The man possessed too much self-control to make

a fool of himself in public, but his cheery face looked stern and lined, as he replied:

"This is indeed news to me, and—are you sure that it is true?"

"One can never be quite sure of anything in this world," replied Mrs. Osborne airily.

"I had no idea of such a thing," said Comstock. He looked ten years older than when he entered Mrs. Quentin's gates.

Mrs. Osborne for once seemed a little frightened. She saw how seriously the man had taken her gossip to heart, and promptly began to shield herself.

"Of course one can never tell whether these rumours are reliable or not,—people do exaggerate so—but everyone seems to fancy they are in love with one another."

"This, then, is the reason why she will not accept my advances," he muttered to himself.

"I only trust that Miss Harlowe will be very happy. She is a girl I have the greatest respect for," he added aloud, at the same time making a movement in the direction of his hostess.

"What? Going so soon?" enquired Mrs. Osborne. "I am sorry; the day is lovely, and the grounds quite exquisite in this sunshine."

"Yes, I am sorry too, but I have an appointment," and so saying the man who had just received a smart blow, bowed with stately courtesy to his tormentor and went home to think over what he had heard.

So thus Mrs. Osborne by her artistic "embroidery" managed to put a temporary stop to David Comstock's matrimonial attentions, though why the woman wanted to do this, she herself did not wait to consider. A general desire to make mischief was probably at the bottom of it, and, also, she was beginning to positively dislike Ursula, solely because she could not find out anything about her.

The buzz of voices sounded cheerful. Every available space in the garden seemed alive with human beings, talking, laughing, and joking together, discussing and criticising their neighbours, to the accompaniment of tea and ices.

"Why, there is Mr. Desmond standing just beside the tulip-tree, talking to that pretty girl in brown," said Lady Ruthven, a matron of thirty summers, with a Napoleonic nose, to her companion, who chanced to be Lady Brandram. "Do you know when he and that girl who plays the violin so exquisitely, are going to be married?"

"You mean Sybil Carlisle. The wedding is to take place soon, I believe."

"I pity her," said Lady Ruthven; "he is such a good man—so very tiresome, you know."

"Personally I think a great deal of Eric Desmond," said Lady Brandram, firing up in defence of her nephew's chum. "He and Hugh are fast friends."

"Indeed! Perhaps I should not express an opinion then, but all the same I am sure he will make a very exacting husband. He gets such alarming periodical fits of moral house-cleaning, and tries to make a clean sweep of our little vagabond sins."

"He is an energetic reformer, certainly, but I do not think his ideas morbid."

"Oh! for the matter of that, everything is morbid nowadays. Have you read Lady Jeune's latest strictures on the smart set? They are vastly amusing."

"No," replied Lady Brandram, "I have not seen the article."

"I have," put in Lady Betty, who, having shunted the curate, came up to join her aunt.

"And so have I," echoed Marmaduke, on the other side.

"To hear you talk, one would really think you were a well-informed person," remarked Betty, snubbingly.

"So I am. I know everything, or pretend I do, which passes for the same thing in society."

Lady Ruthven laughed.

"You are never at a loss, Mr. Myddleton."

"Never," he assented modestly. "I must talk, you know, and if I say a *betise*, what matter? People smile all the same."

"Mrs. Quentin always has such a grotesque collection of people at her garden parties," said Lady Ruthven, scanning through a single eye-glass the groups of men and women congregated under the trees. "Just look at Mrs. Osborne in that audacious dress. What could have impelled her to wear such a youthful garment?"

"No doubt she thinks it charming and a trifle French," said Marmaduke, who never forgot to have a hit at his dearest foe.

"Who is that in the Leghorn hat covered with roses? She looks like an enclosed flower garden," remarked Lady Brandram.

"That is Miss Tatton," replied Ursula. "I was talking to her just now. She comes from some place in Surrey."

"Looks rural enough to give one hay fever," interpolated Marmaduke, "and her boots,—do look at them,"—turning to Lady Brandram. "She must have feet like one of Burne-Jones' virgins."

"Why does not some one write an epic on boots? It would be such a wide field for fancy," said Lady Ruthven. "There are boots that are dreams, boots that are poetry itself—"

"And boots that are hobnailed," said Marmaduke in a sepulchral tone.

"I wish you would not always consider it your duty to romp in and say something startling," laughed Betty.

"To make a fool of myself generally is a passionate intuition with me; I cannot help it," he replied superbly, "but even I may never hope to equal in folly that being who is now on the very apex of triumph."

"Whom do you mean, Marmaduke?" inquired Lady Brandram curiously.

"The Forward Female!" with a flourish of his hand towards Mrs. Quentin.

"Take care; she may hear you," said Betty warningly.

"I do not care," defiantly. "Desmond, I appeal to you," as Eric crossed the lawn and came up to them, "is not the New Woman worthy of being put up in pickle, and preserved as a horrid example for future generations?"

"To make a real success of it, you would have to embalm all her theories as well; they are by far the most important part of her."

"Except her clothes, dear boy," replied Marmaduke. "You forget her knickerbockers."

"If only they would be a little moderate," sighed Lady Brandram, "one might tolerate them more easily; but really so many of them consider it actually clever to be as daring as possible."

"Women whose conversation is as loose as their bloomers, and who think it smart to say indecent things, are not women at all," said Eric sternly. "By their own showing they are unsexed."

"Did I not tell you he was a new broom?" whispered Lady Ruthven into Lady Brandram's ear.

CHAPTER VIII.

> "The world with calumny abounds,
> The whitest virtue, slander wounds;
> There are whose joy is night and day
> To talk a character away."

> "Amid the golden gifts which Heaven
> Has left, like portions of its light, on earth
> None hath such influence as music hath."

THE afternoon had been unusually hot for the middle of June. Women moved languorously and men spoke in lowered voices; for heat in London is distinctly trying.

Lady Brandram ordered the windows to be thrown wide open. If the smuts chose to come in, they could do so, but air she must and would have. So the golden sunbeams streamed over everything and danced a mad reel on the Dutch tulips and masses of geraniums with which the room was filled, turning all to orange and flame-colour with their shining touch.

Mrs. Quentin and Lady Betty had just made their appearance on the scene, fashionably late for tea as usual, and both of them in excellent spirits. What affinity bound the advanced young matron to the essentially worldly little butterfly, people were at a loss to imagine. Possibly their very antipodality accounted in a great measure for their friendship. If asked why she liked Mrs. Quentin so much, Lady Betty would reply that she preferred a woman with some style about her, even if that style were violently masculine, to an everyday sort of person who was totally devoid of *chic*, indulged in Low Church proclivities, or wore large, untrimmed hats.

This latter point was a subject of acute abhorrence to her. A hat, she always contended, was the index to the character of the woman who wore it, and was frivolous, beautiful, poetic, or that most damning of all things—commonplace—according to its owner; but a person who indulged in a straw head-gear of the ungarnished and shady order, must, she insisted, be aggressively respectable—and that meant very dull.

"This season appears to be singularly devoid of match-making," remarked Mrs. Osborne in confidential tones to Lady Brandram, as she munched a macaroon with keen enjoyment.

"Yes, perhaps so. Men are really getting so *blasé*, and so fond of their clubs and their bachelor luxuries, that unless a girl has money or remarkable beauty she runs a poor chance of winning a husband."

"It is such women as that," indicating Mrs. Quentin, who was enjoying herself hugely, and making the staid Mr. Comstock nearly expire with laughter over some racy stories, well told, "who disgust many men with matrimony. They say she positively ill-treats her children—and as to that unfortunate little husband of hers—"

"But, my dear Mrs. Osborne, I scarcely think such

a thing can be true. I have often seen her with Gladys and Mary, and believe me—"

"Of course," interrupting playfully, "I know nothing at all about it; but people will talk, you see, just as they do about Mrs. Wynton. Not that I would repeat it for the world; she is so delightful, I think; but—"

"How do you do, Lady Brandram?"—and Marmaduke Myddleton, smiling as ever, shook hands with the elder lady, thus putting a colon to Mrs. Osborne's discreet inuendoes.

"We were just speaking of your sex," remarked his hostess, "and saying how few men seem to marry nowadays."

"Why do you not start the fashion, Mr. Myddleton?" enquired Mrs. Osborne, gushingly. "There are so many pretty girls of our acquaintance waiting to be wooed and won."

"Mrs. Osborne," replied Marmaduke, "I am no coward, but my bump of reverence is largely developed—at least, so the phrenologists tell me—and when I think of that creature of almost classic fame—a mother-in-law—my reverence turns to awe and takes the concrete form of a wild desire to keep at a safe distance."

"What nonsense! Because you marry a girl you need not also marry her whole family."

"I believe that young men in London think of nothing but their own selfish comforts and amusements," said Lady Brandram seriously, "and would rather spend an evening at the club, or in some music-hall, listening to a Judic or an Yvette Guilbert, than in the society of girls of their own station in whose presence they must put on their manners."

"A form of dress the men of our time especially ignore," said Mrs. Quentin, overhearing the last remark.

"They say the New Man will have to wear petticoats," rejoined Marmaduke solemnly, "and then they will effectually cover up any tatters in his undergarment of manners, just as women's skirts are so often employed as a covering for insolence."

"In what way?" demanded Mrs. Quentin.

"I mean that they often use the accident of their sex to excuse intolerable impertinence; for do we not all know how abominably rude one woman can be to another?" Marmaduke spoke hotly—why, no one exactly understood; it was so unlike him to take anything in earnest.

Lady Brandram felt the strain in the air, and quickly reverted to a former topic. "I do not think men are so degenerated that we need class them all together, and then condemn them with sweeping assertions," she said, in the broad, conciliatory tone people adopt when filling up a conversational breach.

"Or if they have sunk so low in the scale of intellect and power, why do you up-to-date ladies try to prove yourselves their equals? Surely you should have a higher ideal than to rival the very beings you yourselves have torn down from their pedestals and trampled under foot," said Marmaduke, pointedly addressing Mrs. Quentin. But that young person of stalwart notions merely shrugged her shoulders and laughed.

"You could not understand our creed," she replied, "any more than I can understand why you do not marry."

"I'll tell you the reason of that," he said, relapsing into his old, teasing manner. "I love girls, pretty girls, you know, and when they first come out they love me, too—the dear little things, with innocent blue eyes, just like forget-me-nots—and I never do forget them; but they"—and here he heaved a profound sigh—"forget me. By the following season my child-like forget-me-nots have turned into gorgeous yellow blossoms, and, by a process unknown in horticulture, become marigolds. Who am I that I should attempt to vie with an American millionaire, or a toothless earl whose rent-roll is as long as——."

"Your tongue, Marmaduke. Really you talk more nonsense in five minutes than any sane person would in a week," said Lady Betty.

At that moment Sir Hugh came across the room, and joined the group around the tea-table.

"Betty," he said, "I want your advice about some *tableaux* I have been roped in for."

"How delightful! Who is getting them up?"

"Mrs. Ramsay. She means to combine them with a dance."

"What part are you going to take?" enquired Mrs. Osborne.

"Several, I believe, and I want some assistance in the matter of choosing my costumes. One picture is to be out of Lohengrin—rather a difficult period in dress to imitate."

"But very effective if properly carried out," put in Lady Brandram.

"Yes, there is just the rub. Can we carry it out consistently? Betty, have you any portraits of the *preux chevalier* in question?"

An animated discussion ensued, of armour and plumes, silk cloaks and legendary boots, until presently Sir Hugh drew his cousin aside, and together they talked of many things. Ursula and Mr. Comstock, standing in the embrasure of a window, were chatting to all appearances as serenely as well-bred people usually do in society, but in each of their hearts a veritable tempest was secretly raging.

Ursula, full of agonized jealously, watched Sir Hugh and Betty. How they laughed and—yes flirted, for the girl was an arrant little witch, and could no more help flirting, even with her cynical cousin, than she could help living. Once, Ursula saw her put her hand gently on Sir Hugh's arm (she could not know that it was only the pose of a picture they were discussing), and the act sent a spasm of pain through her aching heart. For a moment she thought she must go, then and there, to interrupt them, but pride restrained her; and so she stayed where she was, grasping one hand with the other till the pain of the clench grew almost intolerable. Somehow she gloried in the hurt thus self-inflicted. "What is physical pain to heart pain?" she asked herself.

And the man by her side—he, too, was suffering in a quiet, dignified way of his own, for he fully believed that Ursula was lost to him forever, and the knowledge had struck him with a mortal chill.

What a curious thing society is after all, and what consummate actors and actresses men and women are, more especially the latter, for with breaking hearts brave women will often pursue their thorny way smiling to cover a hideous pain, and with soft, tender words cloak a death-wound.

Suddenly, with the quick reaction of a nature untrained in the narrow ways of conventionality, Ursula turned with a dazzling smile to Mr. Comstock, and, abandoning commonplace topics, talked as a woman only does when her whole soul is in her subject. Here was distinct encouragement, and what man, be he sixteen or sixty, will refuse to return such "sweet discourse of eyes and lips?" Feverishly Ursula played her part, her one thought being to show utter indifference to what was going on at the other side of the room, and recking little in her jealousy how she led on the man of whom she was—hardly semi-consciously—only making a tool to gain her own end.

But the fire soon burnt down, as spurious fires will,

and her better nature asserted itself. It was foreign to her upright character to indulge in the contemptible game of playing off one man against another to the real injury of either, and presently the girl relapsed into her normal manner, and so deliberately threw cold water over Mr. Comstock's freshly raised hopes.

There was another person in the room who had been taking note of the couple seated on the sofa. Mrs. Osborne's ubiquitous lorgnette had been turned upon them more than once.

"What a charming contrast your nephew and Lady Betty make," she remarked vivaciously to Lady Brandram, "She is so winsome and fairy-like, and he as dignified as a Spanish hidalgo."

An audible chuckle from Marmaduke caused her to look round sharply, only to meet two serious brown eyes set in a face devoid of any trace of mirth.

"Betty is a dear little thing," replied Lady Brandram.

"Sir Hugh admires Miss Harlowe very much, does he not?" enquired Mrs. Osborne.

"Indeed, yes, but then we all do that," said Lady Brandram enthusiastically; "so his admiration of her is quite in the fashion, you see."

"Though anyone who had a prior claim upon his affections might reasonably object to such openly expressed devotion to another girl."

"Yes, that is very true."

"I think it might be as well if he did not rave quite so much over this new divinity. People are so ill-natured, you know, and will make remarks, and really anyone with half an eye can see how great his admiration (I might even use a stronger term) is for Miss Harlowe and Mr. Desmond."

With a terrific clash a tall Japanese screen went over just behind the two ladies, bringing down a table as it fell, and smashing to atoms several pieces of bric-a-brac.

"Oh! Lady Brandram, I am so sorry. It was all my clumsiness," and Sybil Carlisle stood there among the *débris* with ashen face and trembling limbs.

The girl had heard every word of the last few sentences uttered between Mrs. Osborne and Lady Brandram, and the final mention of Desmond's name had given her the whole false impression that their conversation referred to Eric instead of, as it really did, to Sir Hugh Galbraith.

"Good gracious, Sybil, is that you? My dear child, have you just come in? Never mind the china," she added, as she saw the girl's look of dismay. "What do a few vases matter? Hugh, ring for Willets to clear the mess away."

"Dear Miss Carlisle, you look as if you had received quite a shock," said Mrs. Osborne, with a honeyed smile. Why do society fiends always inflict their worst stabs with a simper or a caress? Mrs. Osborne had rightly guessed that the cause of the girl's abrupt entrance was the accidental coupling together of Desmond's name with that of Ursula Harlowe.

"Yes," replied Sybil coldly; "I have had a shock; but it is over now, thank you."

"We all get them at times," remarked Mrs. Osborne airily, "but it does not matter much, unless they are of personal moment."

The delicate insinuation conveyed in this speech was not lost upon the girl, and she turned with a quivering gesture to Lady Brandram.

"Pray forgive me," she said, as a child might have begged pardon for some fault committed in passionate self-defence.

"Do not think of it again. It does not signify in the least. Have some tea, dear. Ursula, get Sybil a hot cup. You look as if you needed it," she added with a motherly glance at her.

"Yes, I should like some." But when she got it, the warm fluid seemed to choke her, and she put down the cup still half-full.

During the few moments that the girl sat there, silently sipping her tea while the others fell back into the various conversations which her abrupt entrance had interrupted, thoughts thronged into her mind of little instances when Eric had appeared especially struck by Ursula's beauty,—times when he had spoken of her in warmest praise. Fiercely Sybil remembered them all. This was what they had portended. He, her lover and affianced husband, admired another girl so openly, so deeply, that society talked freely of his attachment to her. It was horrible. What had Mrs. Osborne said?—that "anyone who had a prior claim on him might fairly object to his"—oh—it was too dreadful to repeat even to herself. She turned sick at the mere recollection of that conversation which she had accidentally overheard. Here was an end to his undivided love for her. The blow was all the more keen, because however much they differed on the one point of her entering upon a professional career, in everything else she and Eric had ever been of one mind, and above all other qualities in him, Sybil had most respected his strict moral rectitude of purpose and unflinching code of honour.

Now there was nothing for it but to believe him guilty of treachery towards himself. The thought carried with it a sting sharper than an arrow, turning to bitterness and gall all faith in the man she had promised to marry. It hurt her pride, too, oh! so sorely, that he should have made her the subject of pitying comment to the world, and, have continued to accept her love when—ah!—she remembered it all now: the scene at Mrs. Verner's ball, his agitation on first seeing Ursula, his abstraction later on,—and—he had admitted having known the girl before. Could he by any possibility have once been Ursula's lover? Oh! yes, she understood it all at last. How blind she had been. —What did it matter?—What did she care?

"Sybil," called Lady Betty softly across the room, "when you have finished your tea do play something for us, will you?"

"Leave her alone, Betty," said Lady Brandram; "she looks white and shaken still from that stupid accident."

Sybil glanced up at them with a smile that was born of wounded sensibilities.

"I will play in a few minutes," she said. "That awkwardness of mine made me feel quite nervous for once, but I am all right again now. Will you lend me your violin?" turning to Sir Hugh.

"With the greatest pleasure," he answered. "It's only use is to be of service to you."

"Why do you so seldom play yourself?" she asked, as they turned towards the piano.

He shrugged his shoulders lightly.

"Will you play an accompaniment for me now?" she continued.

"Certainly, if it is anything I know."

"Suppose we try this Nocturne in G.; somehow, I feel like playing it."

He glanced curiously at her as she spoke. Her face was still very white, and underneath her eyes lay dark purple shadows. He fancied, too, that he saw a new expression in them, but had no reason to suppose that it was outraged pride which looked at him through those windows of her soul.

Tenderly lifting the violin to her shoulder and raising the bow, she stood waiting for—she knew not what. "Eric!"——It was the irrepressible cry of a bruised heart. With a touch so light that at first it seemed to be a feeling rather than a sound, she drew out the long, low notes of the prelude—then the waves of rhythmical measure swelled and came gently rolling in, each over-lapping the other; whilst cadences, sad like the moan of the sea, sang, as it were, a soft melody to them.

Sir Hugh was an artist by temperament, and instinctively he caught the inflection of something new, something divine, in Sybil's playing that afternoon; and, with quick responsiveness, he followed her every mood in his accompaniment.

With a sharp crash of the bow across the strings, she plunged into a fresh theme. Her face was pale, her eyes gleamed, a very passion of nervous enthusiasm possessed her, and swayed her lightly. Never before had she played like this. Her lips were parted in a smile, unsteady, unmeant. Like a simoon laden with all the intoxication of the glowing, crimson East, passion-breathing, almost violent in its musical colouring was this *Allegro Appassionata.*

Spell-bound the men and women listened to her as she played out her soul to them. It was a revelation, and yet they did not quite like it, because they did not understand it. On she went with maddening rapture, rushing through the brilliant passages at a speed almost terrifying in its unrestrained pace. Was she a musician, or only an emotional cyclone? Her hearers were holding their breath in the anarchy of sound which encompassed them; they were bewildered, fascinated, and yet repelled, by its *bizarrerie.*

Only Ursula, whose nerves had been on the rack for the past two hours, comprehended its full meaning; for was not she experiencing a similar unbridled pain. Like liquid fire the weird musical phrases scorched her brain and ran through all her veins with the mad intoxication of vodka.

A wild, discordant harmony, an Ibsenish culminating point—and then silence so absolutely dead that it fell like a pall of Cimmerian darkness upon the wrought-up listeners.

Sybil let her arms drop listlessly at her sides, her violin in one hand, her bow in the other, and made no movement to leave her position beside the piano.

"Thank you," said Sir Hugh, as he rose from the music-stool, and at the sound of his voice the spell that bound the audience was loosened, and they came back to earth.

The usual thanks were tendered to the girl, the usual expressions of pleasure indulged in, and then amid a score of leave-takings and hand-shakings and other ridiculous customs of this supposedly enlightened era, Sybil Carlisle slipped quietly away to her own home, bearing the remembrance of past illusions, and passionately forming the deep resolve to throw everything else to the winds and live for her art alone.

A week later she had obtained an engagement with a good concert company to tour in the provinces, and Eric Desmond had received a letter in which she decidedly, and finally, broke off her engagement with him, giving no reason for so doing, but couching her determination in words which admitted of no appeal. Eric called at once to seek a personal interview with her, but was told at the door that Miss Carlisle was "not at home." Then he wrote her a letter begging for some explanation, but it was returned to him unopened. Finally he in his turn grew proud, and so the "little rift within the lute" widened.

CHAPTER IX.

> "Unequal task! a passion to resign,
> For hearts so touched, so pierced, so lost as mine."
> "Ere such a soul regains its peaceful state,
> How often must it love, how often hate,
> How often hope, despair, resent, regret,
> Conceal, disdain,—do all things but forget."
>
> —POPE.

THE line of action pursued by Sybil Carlisle, was, to say the least of it, a very hasty one. To throw over a man to whom she had been engaged for a long time, and for whom she entertained the strongest feelings of love and respect, merely because a notoriously false-tongued woman had uttered some poisonous insinuations against his honour, was almost ludicrous; but in order to understand her conduct in thus summarily dismissing Eric Desmond and snapping asunder all the ties which had hitherto bound them together, one must take into consideration the peculiarly sensitive temperament of the girl.

It made her wince to think of what people were probably saying, of the little hints and slurs in which she felt sure society was indulging at her expense, and she hated her lover for placing her in such a horrible position.

Never for one moment did the girl doubt the truth of what she had overheard. In some things she was singularly childish, for most women, before taking such a serious step, would have sought confirmation of their suspicions; but Sybil neither waited to sift the matter to the bottom, nor listened to anyone's advice. In vain her mother expostulated. The girl was totally unamenable to reason, and flew off at a tangent, determined to follow the dictates of her angry, hurt pride.

Of course, her first instinct was to turn to her violin for comfort; and with a thrill of something akin to pleasure in the midst of her pain, Sybil realized that now she was free to pursue her beloved art, unmolested by any interference from Eric Desmond.

Things do not, however, always resolve themselves just as we expect; and so the girl soon learned, for as the days passed and the sting to her pride grew less sharp, the galling sensation of having been treated with unpardonable insult gave place to a pained regret for her lost love and faith in Eric.

On the very day before Sybil left London, the desire came strongly upon her to see Desmond once more, to tax him, face to face, with his perfidy; and prompted by the faint hope that, after all, he might be able to explain affairs satisfactorily, and prove himself innocent, she was almost on the point of sacrificing her pride and sending for him, when the recollection of Mrs. Osborne's malicious words, sounding again in her ears, turned aside all softer thoughts. The following morning the girl left town, and placed many miles between herself and Eric, and thus the opportunity for reconciliation was lost, no words having been exchanged, nor any outward sign of relenting shown by either of them.

Not only Sybil's mother, but also all her friends, thought this sudden freak on the part of the girl very strange indeed, and numerous were the comments expressed by every one upon her inexplicable conduct. Even to Lady Brandram, Eric's lips were sealed; and Mrs. Carlisle, very tearful and heart-broken, waxed absolutely incoherent whenever the subject was mentioned.

As for Desmond, he was puzzled beyond description, and was naturally very indignant at what he rightly considered a most peremptory action on Sybil's part. No reason given, no excuse offered, but simply a cold, decided letter releasing him, and claiming in return a corresponding freedom from the tie which had previously bound them together. No wonder he was very angry. Then came the final blow to all his hopes of reconciliation. He learned that Sybil had gone on the musical stage and was already a member of the Dolbert Concert company, playing her violin night after night in the provincial towns of the western circuit. At length he fancied he understood it all. It was for the sake of indulging in her passion for the stage—for the sake of pursuing a professional career—that the girl he loved had thrown him over. Had not he and music been rivals for her affection during many a month past? Ah well! He had lost, and Art had conquered. That was the truth Eric thought he had to face.

Two months of continuous travelling and hard work wrought a great change in Sybil Carlisle. Professional life proved by no means the *couleur-de-rose* existence she had pictured it—a sort of New Jerusalem, where all the harps were in tune. Such a fantasy was quickly doomed to be dispelled, for many were the disagreeables and disappointments she had to contend with.

The incessant practice, uncomfortable lodgings and indifferent food, also tried her very much, and though for a time, the excitement of playing before large audiences every night kept her spirits up to the mark, even this stimulus gradually weakened, and she grew daily more heart-sick and miserable. Ambition even seemed to fail her at this point, and with the loss of hope and energy her music began to deteriorate.

Still she struggled on, conscientiously doing her best, and playing with a desperate sort of courage that savoured strongly of despair. By and by, however, the manager began to reprove her in no measured terms for negligence in the execution of certain passages. She did not practice enough, he said, and the public was critical. In vain she worked and strove to do better. Ambition was dead; hope was dead; professional life had lost its glamour.

It was a vastly changed Sybil who came home to her mother in September. She had gone away full of a desire to make her name celebrated. She returned crushed and humbled, having faced some of the sterner realities of life, and done battle with circumstances, only to find herself beaten down, as many another aspirant to fame had been before her. Had the girl embarked upon a musical career under more favourable auspices, she might have achieved great things, for that she had genius was undeniable. But though full of possibilities, like many other artistic people, her temperament was one which could not endure adverse surroundings.

Then, too, as the weeks went by, she began to realize her folly in having so rashly dismissed Eric Desmond. One moment she despised herself for thinking of him so tenderly, when, perhaps, his thoughts were all of another woman; but the next instant she longed for the sound of his voice—for the touch of his strong hand. He had been very dear to her in the past, and time, which softens all things, had drawn a great deal of the bitterness out of her heart.

She began to find excuses for him, to palliate his faults, to even doubt the evidence of her own senses. It was weak, perhaps—but it was very human. In reality she knew of no condonement for his behaviour. Things looked just as black against him as they had done two months before, and yet she could not regard them in the same angry light. Torn in two by conflicting emotions, heart-sick and home-sick, Sybil returned to London early in the autumn, glad to find comparative peace and rest once more.

Eric Desmond, meantime, had plunged into work of a serious nature, giving his whole time and strength to the accomplishment of his Blackfriars scheme, and leading rather a dreary life. Of Sir Hugh he saw but little. The baronet had gone to the Isle of Wight for the months of July and August, and only spent a week in town on his way up north for the shooting.

During the summer the search for Tom Scott was finally abandoned as hopeless, and Sir Hugh, never at any time very keen about the capture of his assailant, seemed quite content to let the affair sink into oblivion. Eric, who pursued the matter rather vigorously at first, had, on reflection, also cooled off in his ardour, thinking, like his friend, that the consequences of a trial might possibly prove very unpleasant to more than one person concerned.

The only further step Sir Hugh took regarding the scoundrel was to write and ask Mr. Harlowe whether he had appeared again in Arleton; but the farmer replied that, as far as he knew, the man was nowhere in the neighbourhood.

Letters had often been exchanged between the baronet and the old man since Ursula had gone to London, and she, too, wrote to her father frequently, and

13

always cheerfully, about her new life and pleasures. Mr. Harlowe was more than satisfied with the apparent success of Sir Hugh's experiment, and each time news of his daughter's increasing beauty and popularity reached him, the simple-minded farmer rubbed his hands with glee and, chuckling softly to himself, "At last she is in her rightful sphere," felt as proud as Lucifer of her triumphs.

CHAPTER X.

"The beginning of the end."

OCTOBER sees many people back in London again. The glories of Homburg and the Engadine have faded; Scotland grows bleak and chilly; from all parts of England there is an influx to the metropolis, and, with a feeling of contentment, town-bred men and women tread once more the pavements of their beloved city.

On a certain night towards the middle of the russet month, it chanced that Herr Mottl was conducting a "Grand Wagner Concert" in the Queen's Hall, which Sir Hugh Galbraith attended in company with several other men whom he had invited to supper afterwards at his chambers.

A queerly assorted sextette they were.

Eric Desmond naturally formed one of the party. Dr. Challotte, the most noted psychological savant of the day, a man famed for his extensive knowledge of hypnotism, was another of the invited guests; whilst the remaining three were: a young guardsman, very much of the Ouidaesque type; Sir Granville-Garton, a lover of the abnormal and a smoker of gold-tipped cigarettes; and Lucien Beck, a pupil of Herr Popper, and already a rising violoncellist.

As they entered the immense hall the overture to

"*Die Feen*" commenced. It was not a concert calculated to entrance the ordinary moderately-musical mind—one must possess something more than that to appreciate Richard Wagner—but, nevertheless, the six men listened attentively, as the celebrated Birrenkoven, Hamburg's idolized tenor, sang "*Siegmund's Lenz-lied*" from *Die Walküre* in an exquisite voice such as has seldom been heard, even in London.

At the conclusion of this number, Sir Hugh drew a long breath. Good music affects some natures to a tremendous extent, and Galbraith's was one of those finely-constructed pieces of mechanism which respond very readily to the influence of sound.

Presently, turning with a leisurely movement to scan the audience, Sir Hugh's roving glance was arrested by the only face which ever had power to hold his attention. Lady Brandram and Ursula were seated at no great distance from him, and again and again did the baronet turn slightly to the left in order to focus his eyes upon the girl. Thus, throughout the evening, he kept continually watching her, drinking in each flickering change of colour, whilst a swarm of thoughts, like the circling of birds at eventide, swept through his brain.

At first Ursula seemed quite unconscious of the severe scrutiny to which she was being subjected, but by-and-by she began to feel uneasy and a trifle nervous. Just then a selection from *Parsival* (that most wonderful of all Wagner's operas) comprising the

Vorspiel, began, and she tried to fix her attention steadily on the orchestra. Lady Brandram, good woman, neither understood nor cared for such involved musical phrases, however excellently they might be rendered, and spent a large proportion of her time watching the audience. Presently she drew Ursula's attention to her nephew and his friends, and as the girl looked straight at Sir Hugh, their eyes met in a concentrated gaze which seemed to draw aside the very curtains of their souls and for the instant made them one.

> " I'll wrestle with the love I cherish'd
> Until in death its flame hath perish'd."

sang a clear soprano voice in the words of "Elizabeth's Prayer." It appeared like the irony of fate. Could it be that a second *Tannhauser* had come into the world, and that his name was Hugh Galbraith ?

It was not until "God Save the Queen" caused a general uprising that Ursula became conscious once more of what was passing around her. The crowd that surged towards the exits seemed to have swallowed up the baronet and his party; but, though the girl did not again see him, Sir Hugh had an opportunity, as the huge assemblage streamed into the street, to point her out to Dr. Challotte.

" There is the most beautiful girl in London," said Galbraith to the old man, with a triumphant smile.

The savant put up his gold-rimmed eye-glass, and

looked earnestly at her; but in another moment she was lost in the crush, and, with a curious puzzled expression of countenance, the doctor turned to his companion.

"Who is she?" he enquired, as if he really wanted an answer and did not merely ask the question from idle intent.

"A young friend of my aunt, Lady Brandram. Miss Harlowe is her name," replied Sir Hugh, pleased that Challotte should be struck by the girl's appearance.

Now, as it happened, it was her appearance which had struck the old man very forcibly indeed, but not at all in the way Sir Hugh imagined. In reply to the baronet's speech he simply grunted, "Umph! Very strange," and there the matter dropped. But if Galbraith had known the groove in which the Doctor's thoughts were running, he would have been utterly astonished and a good deal perplexed.

A first-rate supper, excellent wine, and cigars of finest brand—what more could the heart of man desire? All these Sir Hugh had provided for his guests, who in their turn did full justice to his hospitality; indeed so utterly contented were they that not one of them noticed Sir Hugh's abstraction. During supper the baronet had been the gayest of the gay, but afterwards he grew silent and gradually became absorbed in his own thoughts. Pleasant ones? Yes. None could have been more so, for the sum total of them all was—his experiment.

Presently Galbraith grew a little confused—the luminous ratiocination of his mind dazzled him. Like will-o'-the-wisps the ideas snapped and twinkled before his mental sight—a vivid photograph of Ursula, repellant, exaggerated in outline, stared at him from the beyond. How long he sat there, torn and racked by the awful power within—forcing, compelling, driving him to deeds of undelineated devildom, he could not tell. The past was past and gone; the future held nothing; but the present—ah! that horrible, dominating, insistent present—it was all Ursula.

Just as plainly as he had seen her pure, lovely face at the concert hall, so he saw her distorted features now. Clearer and clearer they grew—more and more distinct. He could even distinguish the colour of her eyes—each thread of ruddy gold in her hair. She was coming nearer—nearer—nearer. Now she was between him and the fireplace. He noticed that he could no longer see a print of Guido's "Ecce Homo," which always hung above the mantle-piece; but, somehow, the crown of thorns just fitted around her head, as she remained motionless before the picture. It was curious that he had never connected her with grief before; yet there she stood with pale, drawn features, wearing, as it seemed, a martyr's aureole of woe.

* * * * * *

"Hugh! Hugh!" burst from the girl's lips. In that moment she was not tragic, she was Tragedy itself. All the men were staring alternately at Galbraith and Ursula. To most of them she was previously known—in fact, to Dr. Challotte alone was she a total stranger—and the horror and amazement of the whole party knew no bounds at her sudden entrance.

Captain Marche, jamming his eye-glass more firmly than usual into his left optic, ejaculated, "By Jove!" and looked as if on the verge of idiocy.

Lucien Beck and Sir Granville-Garton were dumb. The latter seemed in imminent danger of succumbing to a paralytic fit. For once, something really abnormal confronted him, and yet he did not appear to enjoy it. Only two of the occupants of the room expressed any strong personal feelings. Eric Desmond, whose face was stern and set, brought his hand down heavily upon Sir Hugh's arm, and gripping it as in a a vice, thundered, in a tone full of suppressed indignation, "What does this mean?" whilst Dr. Challotte walked hastily across to Ursula. He had been looking intently at Galbraith ever since her entrance, two minutes before, and what the old man read in the baronet's face now caused him to act promptly. Murmuring some soothing words into her ear, he gently led the girl towards the door. Silently and unresistingly Ursula allowed herself to be taken away, for by means of the scientific knowledge at his command, the Doctor understood perfectly how to compel her to obey him.

It was certainly the most astounding case that had

ever come under his notice during the many years in which he had studied medicine, but the old man was far too well versed in the outward signs of a cataleptic state to doubt what was the best mode of treatment in this particular instance. He had perceived, on seeing Ursula in the Queen's Hall, that she was then already slightly under hypnotic influence, and his brief study of Sir Hugh's face and expression when the girl entered the room convinced him that the baronet was responsible for her peculiar mental condition.

Knowing that Galbraith had for some time past dabbled considerably in occultism, the doctor deduced the obvious conclusion that Sir Hugh had willfully subjected Ursula to hypnotic influence. A righteous wrath filled the fatherly breast of the old man at the pitiable sight the girl presented, standing there like a helpless, hopeless child, drawn thither by the unlawfully exercised power of an unprincipled man.

Carefully as possible Dr. Challotte took her home. It was one o'clock in the morning when they reached Belgrave-square. Telling the footman to request Lady Brandram to grant him a few moments' interview, he bade the girl go upstairs to her own room, which she did immediately, unknowing of all that had happened or was even then taking place. To the elder lady the doctor told a plausible story of somnambulism. The girl must have been over-excited, and a fit of sleepwalking had been the result: fortunately, he had found her and brought her quietly back, so nothing need ever be said about the occurrence—better not to tell even Miss Harlowe herself of what she had done. Thus the kind-hearted old man explained, excused and advised, intending to shield Ursula at all events from undeserved scandal, whilst he silently swore to make the perpetrator of this dastardly deed suffer to the uttermost for his wickedness.

Lady Brandram, much upset and anxious about her young charge, thanked Dr. Challotte sincerely for all the trouble he had taken, and, promising to keep silence but at the same time to do all in her power to prevent the girl from getting out of the house again in her sleep, bade him good-night. She went to Ursula's room, only to find her sleeping peacefully, with a faint colour coming and going in her cheeks, her breathing as regular and as easy as a little child's.

No sooner had Dr. Challotte left Galbraith's chambers, taking Ursula with him, than all the men, excepting Eric Desmond, feeling that a storm was brewing in the air, with one accord proceeded to make ready for departure. Sir Hugh, apparently perfectly apathetic, sat in his original position, an eerie sensation of the supernatural deadening for the time being all his other feelings.

Noting the movement of the others, Desmond stepped over to the door and deliberately turned the key in the lock. Then, facing them, he said:

"Pardon me, gentlemen, this affair is not ended yet,

and until Dr. Challotte returns, I cannot permit any of you to leave the room."

Eric knew very well that some explanation must be forthcoming to clear the girl in the eyes of the men who had witnessed her extraordinary entrance, and Dr. Challotte, he rightly conjectured, was the proper person to give such information as would lead to her exoneration; for, though Desmond himself could make neither head nor tail of the affair, he saw that the old scientist had grasped the situation and its remedy. Therefore he determined that no one should leave the place until the doctor came back, as Eric felt sure he would, as soon as he had safely disposed of Ursula Harlowe.

The men looked at one another in surprise when Desmond thus peremptorily addressed them, but eventually accepted the situation with fine unconcern, and sat down again. Eric, after dropping the key into his pocket, commenced a tread-mill up and down the floor, whistling softly to himself an air out of "*The Gondoliers*," and ejaculating "Damn!" at intervals of fifty seconds. Sir Hugh in the meantime grew calmer, and as the first shock evaporated, a little of his customary *sang froid* returned, but still he did not speak. They all seemed to be waiting for something. Presently Dr. Challotte returned and, when Desmond unlocked the door, came in, his eyes fairly blazing with anger.

"You damned scoundrel!" he said, in a low, concentrated voice, to Sir Hugh. "You infernal blackguard! Gentlemen," he continued, turning to the others, who sat bolt upright, curious as to what was going to happen next; "gentlemen, I am known to all of you as a man of some experience and knowledge of psychology. I am an old man, and a perfectly dispassionate arbitrator in this matter. Now, I ask your attention for a few moments. Listen, and believe me when I tell you that the young lady you saw enter this room to-night came here, not of her own free will, not knowingly, nor consciously, but in a hypnotic state, forced here by that vile dabbler in science," with a scathing glance at Sir Hugh, who regarded him coldly, and offered not the slightest protest to his words. "Gentlemen, that unfortunate girl is ignorant at the present moment of what she has done—on that I will pledge my honour; she has simply been the dupe of this experimenter in hypnotism, and I should imagine that this is not the first time she has fallen so completely under his influence."

At this point a sharp exclamation broke from the baronet. He was livid now.

"I am forced to expose your villainy, Sir Hugh Galbraith, unwilling as I am to do so under your own roof; but you leave me no alternative. The stainless reputation of a woman is at stake; and I request you all, as men of honour, to bind yourselves by oath never to reveal what you have witnessed here to-night. Blot it out of your memories; for as there is a God above us I swear to you she is innocent."

A slight stir took place amongst the party as Dr. Challotte spoke thus earnestly, and each one signified his willingness to do as he desired. They were greatly impressed by the old man's forcibility, and Eric Desmond's face was a study of the indescribable.

"As to you, Sir Hugh Galbraith," went on the doctor, "I have known you for a long time as an apostle of the higher branches of science, a cold, cynical man of the world, a being all intellect, with a heart—left out. Now I know you to be a dangerous hypnotist of unscrupulous conscience, a man who has not hesitated to use his power for evil ends, a disgrace to the noble band of psychologists who in faith and uprightness are seeking to turn science to account for the benefit of the human race. Hypnotism is as yet in its infancy, but there are expositors of its blessings whose work is a credit and an honour to the profession at large. Rightly used, it is a great and good power; abused"—with stern emphasis—"it is a degradation."

The old man ceased, and for a few moments silence reigned. Desmond felt as if all things on which he had been accustomed to lean were slipping away from him. Hugh Galbraith a common charlatan! Impossible! And Ursula Harlowe—it was all darkness—he could see no guiding light.

Then the baronet spoke. He had risen to his feet,

his head was thrown back, and his eyes were gleaming with a peculiar lambent light.

"Dr. Challotte," he said, "and you, gentlemen, who have heard me accused, I have only one thing to say before you go. It is this. Of the crime which is laid at my door I declare myself absolutely innocent. It is true that I have studied psychology for many years, but I am no hypnotist. Never once in the whole course of my life have I even tried to exert any hypnotic power." And as the man spoke, his words had a true ring in them which struck his hearers as genuine.

Desmond answered quietly: "Against such a high authority as Dr. Challotte your words are hard to believe. If you did not hypnotize Miss Harlowe, who did? For it must have been done deliberately by someone."

"I do not know; but, I repeat, I did not do anything of the kind."

"Why argue," said the old man to Sir Hugh; "no two men reason alike. It is a question of cerebral mechanism. I saw your features, and I saw your victim's face, and I am prepared to state on oath that you were the hypnotizer and she the subject."

"Dr. Challotte, you are a noted man and your word carries great weight. This is probably the first time in my life I have ever begged a hearing from anyone, but the matter is one of greatest moment; and again, in the presence of you all," with a wave of his hand in the direction of the others, "I swear that I did not on this occasion, and never have in the past, hypnotized Miss Harlowe. Have you no other explanation to offer of the phenomenon?"

"None," replied the doctor conclusively.

"Then all I can say is, that, if I am guilty of this act, I used the force unconsciously."

"Bah! nonsense! Unconscious Hypnotism does not exist—Ah!—wait a moment,—I do recollect once, nearly eleven years ago, hearing of a case in which the hypnotist declared his ignorance of having used any influence; but scientists laughed at the time, and called it impossible,—still—"

Breathlessly his hearers waited for his next words. Desmond, a wild hope springing up in his heart, leaned forward, but Sir Hugh stood still, with folded arms, like a second Andreas Hofer.

A long pause ensued. The doctor seemed to be thinking deeply. At length he went on in a puzzled sort of way:

"It seems quite incredible,—and yet, of course, nothing is impossible in a branch of science of which so little is really known, even by its greatest students and expositors. But Unconscious Hypnotism,—no one has ever dreamed that such a thing existed. Sir Hugh," turning to the baronet, "I should like to say in the hearing of these gentlemen before whom I have accused you of a diabolical trick, that your emphatic denial, coupled with the extraordinary attributes of such a little-understood power, makes it possible (mind

I only say barely possible) that you are an innocent man, and are only, in a latent sense, an accessory to the crime. If it is proved that, in your abyssmal ignorance of this awful and gigantic force, you have stumbled upon the proof of such a factor as Unconscious Hypnotism, the scientific world will owe you an everlasting debt of gratitude, and I shall owe you the humblest apology ever made by man to man. My endeavour will be to prove the truth, but it is a matter requiring much thought and research; therefore, in the meantime, I retract my condemnation, and will only beg you, for all our sakes, to aid me in unravelling this mystery," and with a courtly bend of the head the old doctor departed.

In a body the three other guests rose, and, having given their word of honour to keep silence, bade their host "good-night." They were really rather glad to get out of the over-charged atmosphere, for such an adventure was too uncanny to be pleasant to ordinary-going mortals.

Sir Hugh and Eric Desmond were left alone, both of them in a whirl of conflicting emotions, and each unwishful to be the first to break silence. Galbraith saw many things clearly now in the light of this revelation—this new idea that he had unconsciously hypnotized Ursula Harlowe.

For the first time he understood what the influence might have been which had led her to come to his chambers while he was ill in the previous spring—at least, that was if he could first take for granted his possession and exercise of an unconscious hypnotic force. Several little instances also recurred to his memory which had nonplussed him during his intercourse with Ursula, and which undue power over her on his part would satisfactorily clear up. So the more he pondered on the question the more he inclined to what Dr. Challotte regarded as the "possible explanation" of that night's occurrence.

Eric Desmond, too, rapidly reviewed the past, but the conclusion he arrived at was a much more prosaic one, and before they parted he had broached it to the baronet.

Sir Hugh must send Ursula Harlowe home to her father at once and forever—that was the gist of Eric's cogitations. His friend at first declined to listen to any such proposal, but Desmond's arguments were unanswerable. The fact remained that Sir Hugh had consciously or unconsciously influenced the girl—had, in short, hypnotized her, and would in all probability retain a certain hold over her in the future. This, for Ursula's sake, must be ended as soon as possible, or the consequences might eventually be too horrible to contemplate.

Only once in the course of their argument did Sir Hugh refer to his original scheme, but then and there Desmond turned angry and ruthlessly reviled the whole experiment.

It was very late, or, rather, early before they separated. The eternal tryst between night and day was being kept in the eastern sky, and when Eric walked home in the cool, fresh dawn, he carried with him the baronet's promise to send Ursula Harlowe back to Arleton, a promise he had finally extracted from the unwilling man by threats of exposure unless Sir Hugh complied. "That is the price of my silence," said Desmond decidedly; "take it, or leave it, as you please;" and Galbraith saw discretion was the better part of valour, and gave way accordingly.

It was a terrible wrench to the man to give up the working out of his pet theory. But he saw how black was the case against him and realized that the only reasonable course to pursue at present was a conciliatory one.

CHAPTER XI.

> "My days are in the yellow leaf,
> The flowers and fruits of love are gone,
> The worm, the canker, and the grief,
> Are mine alone."

SLOWLY the hours winged on in their eternal flight, and another day was born for weal or woe. How Sir Hugh hated the growing brilliancy of that glad October morning, as it flooded into the room where all night long he had sat in miserable torture of mind!

No sleep came to rest his tired brain. It was only when the clocks were chiming seven that the baronet arose and went into his bedroom.

As he proceeded to divest himself of his evening clothes, Galbraith paused for an instant to gaze into the long pier-glass, and what that mirror reflected was the index to his mental state. It showed forth a history, and a result. The history was that of the last four hours; the result—capitulation.

A little later on towards the hour of a glorious noontide, the Park was filled with pedestrians and carriages. Riding slowly along the broad, smooth roadway, side by side, were Sir Hugh and Ursula Harlowe, talking calmly of this and that, bowing to passing acquaintances, and exchanging remarks upon various light topics, as they wound their way up the Row towards Kensington Gardens.

Ursula, as unconcerned as a child, felt happy because she rode beside the man she loved, and was quite content to make the most of the halcyon present.

On the baronet's face a very different expression lay shadowed. Was it disquietude, or merely absent-mindedness? Presently they came to a less-frequented part of the Park, and, for a space, conversation drooped. All at once, with a faintly detectable gasp, Galbraith plunged into the subject which had been uppermost in his mind ever since he and his fair companion left Belgrave-square.

"Miss Harlowe," he began abruptly, "have you thought lately of paying your father a visit? I mean—er—of going back to Arleton for a time?"

Ursula turned a slightly surprised glance on him.

"No, I cannot really say that I have."

"It is some months since you have seen Mr. Harlowe, is it not?"

"Yes, but Lady Brandram is so anxious that I should remain with her until Christmas that I have given up all idea of going home just at present."

Sir Hugh felt nonplussed.

"I think, if I may be allowed to make a suggestion, it would be very advisable for you to go to Deepdene in the near future," he said, biting his moustache nervously.

Ursula looked at him curiously. Gently, but with a tact for which few would have given her credit, she questioned Galbraith as to the reasons which instigated his suggestion, and before long had obtained enough information to see clearly that some deep motive had prompted his advice. This both surprised and puzzled her.

"Are you and your aunt tired of me?" she asked, and a note of pathos sounded in her voice.

"Certainly not, Miss Harlowe. Pray, put such an idea out of your head. Why, my aunt is devoted to you!"

"And you? Your reply justifies Lady Brandram, but—"

"Do not misunderstand my words. Your visit to London has been full of pleasure to me, and a continued source of deep interest—"

"Deep interest! Why, Sir Hugh, what a strange way to put it!"

"Not at all. That is just what I mean. Scientifically, you have proved of much—"

A sudden horror came over him. What on earth was he saying? Had last night's fiasco turned his brain to such an extent that he could not control his tongue? Ursula stared at him in amazement.

"Scientifically!" she echoed.

The look of nervous tension in Sir Hugh's face did not escape the girl's notice.

"What do you mean?" she cried impulsively.

He did not answer at once.

A woman's intuitions are very quick at all times,

and, in cases where her love is called into action, they are doubly acute. It took but an instant for Ursula to recollect what sort of man Sir Hugh was. A psychologist *par excellence*, and—she was of scientific interest to him, he had said:

"I mean, Miss Harlowe, that your brilliant career in London society has proved the truth of a theory of mine, that is all."

"What theory?"

"Is there any need to go into the subject further?" queried Galbraith. He was growing most uncomfortable, and cursed his folly in making the careless speech which had aroused the girl's curiosity. "You are the success of the year in Town, and all I suggest is that a short period of rest in the country would be of benefit to your health."

"You are not speaking the truth, Sir Hugh—at least," she corrected herself, "not the whole truth. Tell me what is this theory which you have made use of me in order to prove?" Ursula spoke calmly, and with decision. No one could have guessed of the turmoil that was raging in her heart.

Then Galbraith took a sudden resolution. He determined to accomplish two things at once, namely, to inform Ursula of certain facts and so satisfy her curiosity (which he knew, once raised, would demand an answer before it sank to rest again), and at the same time to make it absolutely certain that the girl should return to Arleton. So he told her of his great experiment.

Mingled horror at the episode of the previous night and fear of its recurrence had made a changed man of Sir Hugh, and, though a week before he would have shot himself rather than bluntly tell the girl that he looked upon her merely as a psychological problem, that morning he was capable of the most brutal lucidity, in order to terminate forever the terrible relations existing between them.

About the fiasco itself he breathed not a word—that, he considered, was too appalling an incident to be even hinted at. It was, indeed, a merciful thing that he so far retained his mental equilibrium as to refrain from telling Ursula anything about the hypnotic element in his scheme, for the utter humiliation of such knowledge, working upon her highly-strung nature, might have led the girl to commit—ah! well—Heaven holds some mercy still for those who are wounded unto death.

"I understand," she said, as he paused after having explained to her briefly, yet clearly, all there was to tell about his experiment.

"You forgive me," he pleaded earnestly, "and are not angry?"

She was silent.

"You can afford to be lenient," he went on, "for you are now on the very pinnacle of social fame."

"And what is that? A pretty iridescent bubble, as thin as it is brilliant."

She seemed to have grown years older during the last half-hour, and worldly-wise too.

"That may be the opinion of pessimists, but men and women think differently."

"Women love society, but they love—other things more—honour, for instance, and chivalry."

Sir Hugh wondered if this was meant for sarcasm. A mighty change, indeed, had swept over Ursula as she listened to Galbraith's cold, hard definition of their relative positions during the past year, each word falling like a stinging lash upon that quivering thing, a woman's heart, sore with unreturned love. First she felt numb, and then cynical. But only for a few moments. Presently a gentler intonation coming into her voice, she said:

"Let me understand it all. You wanted me to be a subject for the establishment of one of your pet theories, and now that the answer is proven, you have finished with me—I am no longer needed here; I can go home."

Sir Hugh quaintly realized how logical were her arguments, and yet what a horribly mean and cruel truth they contained. He did not dare to contradict the girl outright, for he could not tell her of the paramount reason why she must go away from London, and from—him. The dabbler in psychology was already tasting of the Dead Sea fruit.

"Do not put things so bluntly, Miss Harlowe, and I beseech you, do not take the matter so seriously. Believe me, you are indulging in an exaggerated view of things."

"Could any thought of mine magnify the extent of your experiment? I am sorry it has ended so unfortunately for me, but then there are a great many things in life one is sorry for—that is only human nature," and a wan smile flickered across her face.

A strained look had grown within her dark eyes, and there was a weary drooping of the curves about her mouth. With a rush there came back to the girl vivid memories of the past winter, spring, and summer; like the ghosts of a buried year they trooped out to surround her in her hour of sorrow. Ah! how fragrant had been the dawn of love, and now all that remained to her was the pale mocking spirit of reminiscence, the miserable make-believe of the present.

She had known that her love was unrequited; she had known the halcyon dream could not last forever; but to end thus—slain in an instant.—ah God!—it was cruel! Why had not Sir Hugh pretended friendship for her a little longer? Now—she must let him go—at once and forever. Ah! yes, before she became odious to him. Perhaps then he would think of her sometimes with—regret.

"Is it anything I have done," she questioned at length wistfully, "which has caused you to suddenly tell me all this?"

In view of recent developments Galbraith felt thoroughly ashamed as she thus questioned him.

"No, Miss Harlowe. There is really nothing to be so serious about. It is only that I think it will be advisable for you to go back to your father for a time. Do not leave us too suddenly—such an action on your part might raise comment—but perhaps next week—"

"Very well," she answered coldly, "I will go home—next week."

Slowly they turned their horses' heads homewards, and as Ursula rode silently beside the man who had been her idol for so long, all the love in her heart welled up in a mighty fountain, and her throat ached with the muttered words she would fain have poured out at his feet.

Galbraith despised her! No sooner had this idea formed itself in her mind than she felt an unalterable conviction that it was true. What was she after all but a hollow sham, the product of a false civilization. She was nothing but a farmer's daughter. All this new, smart life was a hypocritical farce, and she herself only a bubble on the bosom of the social river.

With a strangled sob of despair, she said to herself, "He despises me because I am a living lie!"

CHAPTER XII.

> "I shall go my ways, tread out my measure,
> Fill the days of my daily breath
> With fugitive things not good to treasure,
> Do as the world doth, say as it saith;
> But if we had loved each other——O sweet,
> Had you felt, lying under the palms of your feet,
> The heart of my heart, beating harder with pleasure
> To feel you tread it to dust and death."

How the remainder of that day passed Ursula Harlowe never exactly knew.

The deep, sweet dream of her life was past. Dead were all the joys of yesterday which had sprung up only to be ground down under the heel of a cynical, selfish man. It was her misfortune, not her fault, that she had loved, but too well, a being who was not worthy of the high pedestal upon which her whole-souled devotion had placed him.

No one was more thoroughly capable of keeping her own counsel, however, than Ursula, and bravely did the girl go through the long, trying afternoon and the even more trying dinner-hour which followed it. Fortunately, Sir Hugh, actuated perhaps by some lingering sense of shame, kept away from his aunt's house for the remainder of the day, and thus the girl was spared the pain of being forced into contact with the man who had just killed, at one blow, her self-respect and her pride.

The shock of learning, so suddenly, that she was to Galbraith merely a psychological experiment, a sham foisted upon society simply for the purpose of proving a vague theory; and also of discovering that he had never regarded her as anything but a beautiful fraud, his inferior, and the puppet of his idle moments, had been nearly sufficient to unhinge the girl's mind, and the very calmness she displayed all through that day was only another evidence of the tension to which her nerves were strung.

In spite of all that had taken place, the baronet's coolness soon re-asserted itself, and after spending a few hours in aimlessly doing nothing, he proceeded to hunt up Eric Desmond at the Club, and complacently inform him that everything was settled—Ursula Harlowe was going home, and so all disastrous consequences would now be safely avoided.

It caused Sir Hugh no small amount of astonishment that Eric did not appear very satisfied upon the subject.

"What on earth do you want more, my dear fellow?" demanded the baronet, in response to the somewhat dubious look upon his friend's face.

"Because you are so blind do not imagine, Hugh, that all the world is blind also. You are not out of the wood yet."

Galbraith shrugged his shoulders.

"As the old Quaker said to his wife, 'All the world is queer but thee and me, and even thou art a little queer.'"

"It may be so. Perhaps the old man knew more of human nature than we give him credit for. But it appears to me that you are by no means so secure from the consequences of this scrape as you suppose. A great wrong has been done, and the results of it must be felt some day or other."

There were many things which troubled Eric just then. His own private affairs were all topsy-turvy. Sybil Carlisle and he were still as far apart as ever, and this, coupled with all his anxiety about Ursula and Galbraith, had served to darken the man's life for the time being with a cloud of anxiety which showed no silver lining.

By-and-by the day wore on to a close; with noiseless steps, and wrapped in a cloak of shadow, the gentle October eventide passed through the land, while the twinkling stars came out one by one to watch her timid progress.

Ursula Harlowe sat alone at last. The ordeal and strain of keeping up appearances was over, and she was once more at liberty, in the privacy of her own room, to cast all restraint to the winds.

There is a subtle atmosphere which clings about an apartment belonging exclusively to a woman. The inanimate objects therein seem in a sense to receive the impress of her individuality; perhaps this is because there, and there alone, she permits herself to indulge in the luxury of being perfectly natural. At any rate the room in which Ursula sat that night was essentially of a refined type, and bore traces of the girl's tastes in the various books and objects lying scattered about it. A wood fire crackled on the hearth; and, throwing herself into a chintz-covered arm-chair before its cheerful blaze, she gave herself up to the task of sorting her ideas and putting her mind in order.

Slowly, and speech by speech, the girl went over the whole conversation which had taken place between herself and Sir Hugh. Each wounding insinuation he had spoken, each fresh revelation of what had been the real state of affairs for months past, came back to her now with a cruel distinctness. Thus she pondered on all that had occurred in the by-gone time which had been so full of light and love, but which was now merged into eternity, never to come back again.

Oh! the sadness of that aftermath! Gently she took all her girlish hopes and laid them in a grave, deep down in the dusts of despair.

Like a scarlet poppy her love had blossomed through the summer tide of its existence; but now that was all over. Cut down by the hand of a ruthless man it had died and withered, soon to be buried under the mould of oblivion; only perchance in the land of eternal spring might that glorious flower ever bloom again.

Like a lost angel, wandering in search of the spirit

of humanity, Ursula waited dumbly where the fumes of Hell tarnished the golden fringe of Heaven.

Then all at once a laughing sob of anguish broke from her lips, more normal in its intensity than the deadly calm which had preceded it.

"What does it all matter? What does anything matter?" she cried in her misery. Vaguely the girl understood that something beautiful had been burned out during that long purgatorial vigil. It was the Christ-like faith of a little child which died that night in her bruised heart.

And when the dawn crept in through the shutters, a tiny beam of sunlight fell tenderly on the bowed head and shoulders of the girl who knelt there bent to earth in humble penitence and prayer.

Sir Hugh Galbraith had murdered the love of Ursula Harlowe.

CHAPTER XIII.

> "Let this be said between us here:
> One love grows green when one turns grey:
> This year knows nothing of last year;
> To-morrow has no more to say
> To yesterday."

"AND so you really wish to go home, my dear?"

"Yes, Lady Brandram, for a little while, at any rate," and as she spoke an indescribable smile stole round about the corners of Ursula's mouth.

"Well, of course you shall please yourself, child, but, I confess, I am sorely disappointed," replied the elder lady, as she passed her hand lovingly over the girl's ruddy hair. "If you would only remain here until Christmas I should be more content."

Ursula was sitting on a low stool resting her head against the arm of a chair. Evening had fallen before the occupants of the room grew aware of the lateness of the hour, but still Lady Brandram did not ring for lights to be brought, and so the two women talked on confidentially in the oxydized-silver twilight.

"You have been so kind to me that I feel almost guilty in running away so hurriedly, but" (and here a trembling of the lips caused the girl to turn her face slightly towards the window) "I get such a longing for home sometimes—and Daddy," with another quiver, "that nothing will do—except"—

"I know, my child. It is only natural, after all, and Mr. Harlowe has been very good to spare you to us for so long. But, Ursula, have you been happy here?" with a quick impulse of tenderness in look and tone.

"Always, with you, dear Lady Brandram. I can never thank you enough for your kindness to me; and please do not think me ungrateful because I say that I want to go home now."

"What nonsense! Just as if everybody did not, or, at least, ought not, to love their home the best of all places in the world. Try, though, not to forget us altogether; but when you have stilled the heimweh, come back to me for another visit. Promise that you will do this, Ursula, and then, I shall be more willing to let you go."

"From the bottom of my heart I promise that, replied the girl; for she thought of how some day, when Sir Hugh should be away from London, she would dearly love to return for a time to the kind old lady who had been like a second mother to her during the past year.

"There is another thing," she went on, "which I very much wish to do, that is, if you have no objection to the idea. Sybil Carlisle and I have always been such great friends that I want to go and stay with her for a few days before leaving for Arleton."

This plan Lady Brandram readily agreed to, but she little guessed that a strong wish to avoid Sir Hugh Galbraith underlay the girl's proposition,

Thus it was settled, and no one rejoiced over the prospect of the brief companionship more than Sybil, for she was very lonely in those days, and having long since discovered that Ursula, at all events, was totally innocent of having ever flirted with Eric, however much he might have erred in that direction, she entertained exactly the same warm feelings of friendship for the farmer's daughter as before. Sir Hugh was also a trifle relieved when he heard of the new plan; for, truth to tell, he wished to avoid Ursula quite as much as she desired to avoid him. So that the only person who felt any lingering regret over the fact that the girl would not spend the few remaining days of her London visit in Belgrave-square was Lady Brandram, who, dear, unsuspicious old soul, hummed on her kindly way, totally oblivious of the tragedy which was being worked out before her very eyes.

One person who hailed with positive joy the arrival of Ursula at the Carlisle's house was David Comstock. Quite recently it had come to his knowledge that all the gossip told him by Mrs. Osborne regarding the existence of an engagement between Sir Hugh and the belle of the season was entirely false, and accordingly his spirits went up to bubbling pitch, and his attentions became correspondingly ardent.

On the very day that Ursula went to her new destination he called, and had the good fortune to find find her at home. This visit, a lengthy one, was only the prelude to many others, and right glad was the elderly lover that he now had a chance to woo the girl under the roof of Mrs. Carlisle—anywhere, in short, rather than at a house where Sir Hugh Galbraith (whom he had erstwhile looked upon as his successful rival) had the unchallenged *entrée.*

There was a faint balm to the girl's wounded heart in this complete devotion lavished upon her by Comstock, and though she never dreamed of reciprocating his love, still, to know that there existed some one who cared for her, anticipated her slightest wishes, and in all things made her his first consideration, was a very soothing feeling.

It turned out as might be expected, Mr. Comstock proposed and was accepted. Marriage with a man like David Comstock meant safety from all the slurs and misunderstanding on the part of the persons with whom Ursula had been moving in London.

Had Ursula not been tortured beyond endurance for the last few days, and at the very instant when Mr. Comstock proposed to her, felt desperate as only a heart-broken woman can, she would never have consented to become the wife of a man for whom she entertained nothing but feelings of indifference. Marriage with a man like David Comstock meant safety from the slurs of female society gossips; and more than that, it meant a new, tenable position in the world. When a woman loses her mental balance she will act with inconceivable rashness, neither caring that she hurts another, nor recking what the future will inevitably bring to her.

When Mr. Comstock said: "Ursula, I love you. Will you be my wife?" she had stood as if turned to stone, and as he pleaded in honest, outspoken words, encouraged to do so by her silence, she turned upon him a look of such utter weariness that involuntarily the man put an arm around her waist and drew her head down upon his shoulder.

"I am very wrong to let you do this, to even listen to you," she murmured, "but somehow I have lost all power of resistance. I am so tired."

Then he pressed her closer to him and tenderly asked the old, old question: "Will you not love me a little, darling?"

She replied: "I do not love you, but, if you wish it, I will marry you."

It was not a very sentimental answer, but David Comstock was satisfied.

No thought of triumph over the baronet found place in Ursula's mind when she took the vigorous step of accepting David Comstock. It never struck her that she could in future defy the man who had hitherto considered her beneath him, or that in her new position she would stand on the same social level as Galbraith himself. Her only idea was that now she would be safe from detection, sneers and humiliation, and, above all, safe from the power of the society fiend.

CHAPTER XIV.

> "Yet the first bringer of unwelcome news
> Hath but a losing office."

> "I have seen the desire of mine eyes,
> The beginning of love."

THE next day Ursula sent Lady Brandram a note telling her briefly of her engagement to Mr. David Comstock. It was late in the day when the note reached her, and its effect was startling. She felt that she had been a party to a deception, and she dreaded the result of a disclosure. As a consequence Lady Brandram passed a very restless night. She rose on the following morning with the full determination to get the unpleasant business before her over as soon as possible. As soon as she had finished breakfast, she sat down and wrote a note to her nephew, summoning him to Belgrave-square immediately on "a matter of the greatest importance."

L'homme propose but things never do turn out just as they should; and by a series of mischances, mere trifles in themselves, and yet, when banded together, strong enough to upset the "best laid schemes o' mice an' men," Sir Hugh did not receive his aunt's letter until twelve o'clock. Deeming from her words that something serious was afoot, he drove as quickly as a hansom could take him to Lady Brandram's house, and there found her in a state of considerable anxiety over his non-appearance.

"I am so sorry, aunt, that there was a mistake about your note; I got it only just now at the Club."

"Never mind; you are here at last, and that is the main point. Something dreadful has happened, at least it may still prove all right, only you must go at once and tell Mr. Comstock all about it."

"My dear aunt, what are you talking of?"

"Oh! you must try and understand; it is so urgent."

"I will if you tell me what it is that has taken place."

"Ursula has sent me a note telling me of the whole affair, so I am sure it is true. Mrs. Osborne said it was utterly impossible, and that it was my duty to inform him. And really, Hugh, I am afraid——."

"Now, aunt, look here, how can I do anything to help you unless you explain yourself a little more clearly? Repeat to me what it was Ursula said to you."

"She—oh! Hugh!" and here Lady Brandram began to get confused again, "she never thought, I suppose, of all the dreadful consequences—but you must put things straight for her."

Sir Hugh was growing a little nervous, and fast getting to the end of his patience.

"Ursula Harlowe told you—what?" he asked, very sternly.

"That she was engaged to Mr. Comstock," faltered Lady Brandram.

Here was a pretty kettle of fish! Galbraith had often laughed at Desmond for predicting evil and always looking on the worst side of things, and now the realization of all Eric's worst prognostications had come true.

Sir Hugh was literally overwhelmed at the unlooked-for piece of news. In the past he had scoffed at the notion of Ursula's unworthiness to wed with a gentleman; but recent events had considerably changed the current of his ideas on this subject, and he now saw the full significance of Desmond's objection to deceiving society on the score of the girl's antecedents. To marry a woman of *bourgeoise* extraction, with your eyes open to the risk, was one thing—to do so in ignorance of her birth was quite another matter.

For a few minutes the baronet vouchsafed no further remark than that first involuntary ejaculation. He felt a little sick, as strong men do in times of severe mental emotion, and he thought great, bitter, repentant thoughts.

Under the influence of his outward calmness Lady Brandram grew less nervous, and presently she went on to tell him what she considered it was his duty to do. Sir Hugh quietly acquiesced in her proposition, promising to go directly after luncheon and tell David Comstock the entire story.

With what feeling of shame and lashings of conscience Galbraith started on his way to Upper Brooke Street, no mortal ever guessed. Oh! the rottenness of that Dead Sea fruit! How it revolted him now! The sin, the fraud, the hollowness of his experiment! Was this, indeed, the end? Surely it must be. Life could hold no purgatorial abyss so deep as this task before him.

He wondered vaguely why he had so readily consented to abase himself before a man whose respect and friendship he had hitherto enjoyed; but, all the same, there he was bowling rapidly along to David Comstock's house, with the fixed determination to make confession.

"Is Mr. Comstock at home?"

How easy it was to ask this simple question, how common-place to follow the butler up to the drawing-room, and there stand by the window, looking out at the passers-by. Sir Hugh gave the skeleton of a laugh. Here was he in Comstock's house, waiting to kill all the man's hopes of love and happiness, all his faith in womanhood, all his—

The door opened with a creak, and David entered. Advancing slowly he motioned Galbraith to take a chair, but did not proffer his hand in greeting. The two men regarded each other steadily, and opened up a fire of brief sentences, meaningless, and obviously without point, like two opposing elements mustering up their forces for the attack.

Presently, rising to his feet, Sir Hugh gripped the

back of a chair with fingers that showed white at the knuckles from over-tension. Then he began to tell the truth. It seemed as if he were reeling off a lesson learned by heart.

"Is that all?" asked Comstock, as the baronet ceased speaking.

"Yes, that is all, so help me God!"

"I am glad of your corroboration, Sir Hugh. It is an added testimony to the truthfulness of—Ursula."

"She has told you—"

"All."

"But when?"

"Last night. Do you see this letter?" drawing an envelope out of his pocket. "It was handed to me during the evening, and was written by a man named Tom Scott. Who he is I have since learned from my late *financée*," with a slow smile, "and I gather that baffled jealousy prompted its composition."

Sir Hugh stared at the man before him. How calmly Comstock took it all!

"I see you do in truth know everything," said the baronet; "all that remains for me to do, is to ask your pardon for the deception of which I have been the cause, and you the victim."

"I can well afford to forgive you now, and I do so freely, but remember, Galbraith, the tie of friendship is severed between us forever."

Sir Hugh bowed silently. He felt the justice of David's words.

" When a man makes license the definition of liberty, as you have done, he voluntarily places himself outside the pale of good fellowship."

The baronet bowed again coldly; he could answer nothing.

" I think I need not detain you any longer," said the stockbroker.

Then something awakened in Galbraith's mind.

" Miss Harlowe," he stammered, " does she—have you told her—I mean she will go home at once—I suppose—"

" That will be for her to decide."

" You have broken off your engagement already, then ? "

" You have absolutely no right to ask such a question, but I will answer it nevertheless. Miss Harlowe and I are no longer engaged. Ursula is my wife."

" Wife ? "

" Yes," we were married this morning, and she is already in her own home."

Stepping across to a door leading into the library, he opened it, and in another instant had led Ursula in by the hand.

" Allow me to present to you Mrs. Comstock."

The effect was electrical. Sir Hugh looked up startled. It was like the coming of an angel unawares. He murmured something, he knew not what. They were in the presence of the catastrophe of three lives.

From that instant Galbraith experienced a new sensation—the first, great, grand, absorbing passion of his life. He loved—and knew to his everlasting desolation—that the woman he must love for evermore was—Ursula.

Too late, too late! In that beautiful by-gone past all had been laid at his feet, and he had not deemed it worth the gathering up. Now, when hope was denied to him, he loved to the uttermost.

BOOK III.

THE EXPERIMENT IS ENDED

" Now thou art gone beyond thought's utmost reach,
Beyond the joy we knew, the love, the pain,
Out on the dim dark way.
The problem is resolved for thee, but I,
Crushed, questioning, despairing, still remain,
And nothing thou wilt say.
Is love so weak thou dost not heed my cry?
Is memory so vanishing, so vain,
That death wipes all away?"

—W. W. S.

CHAPTER I.

"Fabrum esse suæ quemque fortunæ."

PSEUDO-SALLUST.

THE whirligig of time, which stops for no man, had swirled on through summer and winter, storm and sunshine, until several more year-cycles were spun off into eternity.

Three years had come and gone since the day on which David Comstock married Ursula Harlowe—years of comparative peace to both husband and wife, for in all honour and faith the girl did her duty towards the man whom she had so rashly wedded. Though his firm belief that some day she would learn to love him was never realized, her quiet genuine affection satisfied David to a very considerable extent.

Love was dead for Ursula in this life, but she gave, as a substitute for it, a perfect devotion to her husband's interests, all the more punctilious because it was the outcome of duty, and not of tenderness.

Two other marriages had also taken place within a year. One, that of Sybil Carlisle to Eric Desmond, and the other between Lady Betty Mornington and a curate of ritualistic tendencies, a man of excellent family, but penniless. This latter couple were as happy as young married people are proverbially supposed to be, and in spite of the prospect of straightened means, appeared perfectly contented. Matters might not have gone so smoothly in the future, however, if Lady Brandram had not luckily come to the worldly rescue of Betty and her husband, and insisted that they should make their home with her.

With Eric and Sybil things also went very well, somewhat to the surprise of Mrs. Carlisle, who, knowing all the past struggles between her daughter and Desmond over the question of art, experienced some serious misgivings regarding the continuance of a truce; but as the months rolled by, and peace still reigned supreme, her fears gradually sank to rest.

And Sir Hugh Galbraith, what of him? Outwardly he was the same cold, cynical man of the world, but inwardly, ah! what a change had been wrought there. From the moment in which he first realized that he loved Ursula with all a man's passionate devotion, his entire life had been altered. Habitual custom, cultivated to a point of perfection, kept his external conduct invariably impassive; only to himself was known the regret, the remorse, the gnawing, burning pain of desolation. In deepest sorrow he mourned the colossal loss of his life, the one great opportunity of happiness which Providence had given to him, and which he had neglected to grasp until it was snatched from under his very eyes by another man.

Only very occasionally did Sir Hugh ever meet the Comstocks; indeed, he purposely avoided them as much as possible, for the double reason that he could not bear to see Ursula as the wife of another man and that he still felt a lurking fear of the recurrence of some hypnotic phenomena. Then, too, Comstock had never renewed his former cordial relations with Galbraith, and the latter gladly allowed the breach between them to widen. Knowing that his love for Ursula was hopeless, he dreaded the power within him, as men fear an evil spirit.

For a considerable time after that terrible night when Dr. Challotte had with scathing words denounced him as a charlatan of the lowest type, the baronet, with much help from the old scientist, strove diligently to unravel the mystery which surrounded the incident; but though, together, the two men had travelled intellectually a great way since that eventful evening, they seemed to come but little nearer to a fuller comprehension of the truth. There are some problems which even to the most learned and enlightened must always remain unsolved, and this appeared to be one of them.

Whether in the years to come Unconscious Hypnotism will ever be established as a recognized power, who shall say? Psychical research is yet in its infancy, and at present no one dare affirm what may or may not be within the bounds of possibility. Basing his studies upon the evidence supplied to him by Sir Hugh Galbraith's experience, Dr. Challotte did all that scientific rules permitted in order to attest the new proposition; and so far as he went the theory looked plausible enough in the abstract, but the old man utterly failed to demonstrate it practically. Personally he believed in the baronet's affirmations, and completely exonerated Sir Hugh from all charge of dishonourable conduct. Yet there he had to stop, for further than that he could not, dared not, pronounce definitely. As the world was fortunately in perfect ignorance of the unprecedented occurrence, Galbraith's public position was in no way affected by this non-approval of his defensive explanation.

At the end of three years all effort to establish Unconscious Hypnotism on a sound psychological basis having failed, Dr. Challotte gave up the quest in despair; but, though Sir Hugh never to the end of his life quite abandoned all hope of verifying his suspicions, no answer to the hypnotic problem was ever forthcoming. So, whether or no the baronet had unconsciously hypnotized Ursula Harlowe, whether her love for him was inspired by his dominating power, or whether that power was engendered by her love for the man himself, who can tell?

CHAPTER II.

"The story of her birth."
—ADDISON.

EARLY in November, just three years and a month after the date of his marriage, David Comstock was killed in the hunting field by a fall from his horse. Exactly how the accident happened no one ever learned. But there was a nasty stone wall with a big ditch on the off side; man and animal rose to it; then followed an instantaneous crash, and a riderless horse galloped away over the fields, leaving behind in that deep, slimy ditch an insensible human form. Before the end of the day David was dead.

This all took place down in Wiltshire, just at the commencement of the hunting season; and when the blow fell, Ursula's first instinct was to go back to her old home in Arleton, where she knew a loving welcome from her father always awaited her.

In more ways than one it had all been a terrible shock to the girl, for as the months came and went, she had by degrees learned to depend upon David's kindly protection and unfailing goodness. When such a violent termination was put to his life the young widow felt unspeakably lonely and crushed, missing at every turn the thoughtful and affectionate care with which Comstock had always surrounded her.

Mr. Harlowe was naturally extremely glad to have his daughter at Deepdene. Life had been very solitary for the old man ever since Ursula went to London, and now, after years of constant separation, the farmer appreciated keenly the companionship of the girl he loved so dearly. For some weeks all went on in a quiet way. November gave place to December, and the year was fast approaching its dissolution before Mr. Harlowe finally made up his mind to do a certain thing which he had come to regard in the light of an imperative duty.

One night, shortly before Chistmas, he and Ursula were sitting in the oak parlor before a blazing hearth, the girl's one idea being to get as close as she possibly could to the fire, without being in the absolute conflagration, for the night was very raw. Outside the rain fell like tears of sorrow dropped from the eye of Heaven over the fields which lay stretched out under a low-arched sky, mist-mantled and desolate, silent, save for the creaking of naked branches as the wind sobbed through the trees and chased a mass of grey clouds across to the dim horizon.

No matter how we struggle against it, our thoughts are constantly subservient to the weather. And so it was with Ursula on that particular winter evening. She felt unusually dreary; even conversation had temporarily languished between herself and her father, and during a short spell the moaning of the wind, as it rose and then died away in a plaintive wail, was the only accompaniment to the girl's vague fancies. Presently Mr. Harlowe spoke.

"Ursula," he began, and the spasmodic jerk with which he brought out her name, while it was really only the natural outburst of an over-burdened mind, sounded forced to the girl's ears, "Ursula, it has come to me very strongly of late that I did not act rightly by you when I let you go to London four years ago."

"Why, father?" she queried, looking up at him in surprise.

"For several reasons, the chief one being that you went there in ignorance of a fact which you had a perfect right to know.

"I also did a wrong to Lady Brandram, and to Sir Hugh Galbraith at the same time," went on the farmer, "and I did an even greater wrong to your poor husband, my dear. There now, don't you cry," for at the mention of David, the tears, already so near to the surface, welled up in the girl's eyes. "But, lass, if I had it all to do over again, I would tell the truth from the beginning."

The old man paused and Ursula cried on quietly. She was feeling unstrung that night, and somehow she missed her husband's strong arms, which had always been her shelter against every trouble.

"I want you to listen to me, my girl," said Mr. Harlowe earnestly, "while I tell you a story of things which happened many years ago, long before you were born."

"Yes, Daddy, go on."

The farmer looked at her sadly.

"Do not call me 'Daddy' again until you have heard what I am going to say; after that, if you still wish to do so, you can continue to call me by the old name."

"Nothing will ever alter my love for you, father," replied the girl, affectionately stroking his arm; "but go on."

"Three and twenty years ago," pursued the old man, "I married your mother. Ah! Ursula, she was a lovely girl herself then, just about your age, and like you, my dear, a widow."

"A widow?"

"Yes, and with one child, a little girl."

"And the child was—" she paused, and stared at Mr. Harlowe with bewildered eyes.

"You, Ursula. Yes, you were just twelve months old when I married your mother, and so, you see, I am not your father at all, though you have always called me by that name. And indeed I have loved you, lass, as if you had truly been of my own flesh and blood."

Ursula felt too amazed to speak, and the old man continued:

"I want to explain to you a little bit why you never heard of all this before. You see your real father, your mother's first husband, was—a rascal; I am sorry to have to tell you this, my dear, but it cannot be hidden any longer. He was a young nobleman, belonging to a well-known family, who fell in love with your mother during her first season, and induced her to run away with him. She was very fond of Lord Wyvern at the time, but her people would not hear of the match taking place, and when she took the law into her own hands and fled across the channel with the handsome young ne'er-do-weel, her father and mother refused to forgive her for marrying such a scamp. After some months spent in wandering about the continent, the young couple drifted to Monte Carlo, where Lord Wyvern took to his old habits of gambling; staking all his available cash on the green tables, until he and his poor little wife were reduced to abject poverty, for fortune distinctly refused to smile upon his ventures at cards. Then you were born, Ursula, in a small town near Marseilles, and shortly afterwards your father was killed, shot in a disreputable gambling fray,"—and here the old man's voice quavered.

"Oh! my child," he continued in broken tones "pray Heaven you may never know the terrible misery which your dear mother endured in those dark days. She came to Arleton when you were only six months old, ruined in health, a sad-eyed woman of twenty-three, her one desire being to bury herself where her relations could never trace her. They had deliberately cast her off, and she never, to the day of her death, would sue to them for forgiveness. Well, I fell in love with Isobel Wyvern, and we were married. When I look back on the perfect happiness of those two short years of our wedded life, I thank God, Ursula, that he gave me so sweet a wife.

"When she was taken away she left me a little blessing in you, mere baby though you were, and begged me, as she lay dying in my arms, never to tell her sad history, or the truth about your parentage, to any living being, unless it were absolutely necessary. You see, child, I kept my promise to her; but I fancy sometimes that it would have been better if I had told you this story a few years ago."

Ursula sat wrapped in deepest reflection. The tale she had just listened to was so startling, and meant so much to her. Ah! yes, how much—how very much it did mean.

"Then you are, after all, no relation of mine whatsoever, Daddy; but how good you have always been to me," said the girl gently, "just the same as if you had been my real father."

"I loved you at first for your mother's sake, child, but by and by I grew to love you for yourself alone. You were a sort of legacy from my dead Isobel, and I cared for you as her baby, until you crept into my lonely old heart, and made it warm once more. In the end I came to look upon you as the sunshine of my life and home."

"Dear Daddy," said Ursula, as she fondly rubbed her cheek against his hand, while all the time her thoughts were running in one direction.

"My father was Lord Wyvern," she mused, "a gentleman of good birth, and my mother—" "Daddy," she said aloud, "Who was my mother?"

"Her name was Isobel Mornington. She was a younger sister of Lady Brandram."

"And you never told Lady Brandram who I was?"

"No. It is for that I now blame myself so severely. I see it was a deceitful thing to do—to let you go to her as a stranger, when you were in reality her own niece."

"Then if I am Lady Brandram's niece, Sir Hugh Galbraith must be my cousin."

"Certainly, though I never knew of the circumstance myself until he brought me a letter from his aunt asking you to go to London; for your mother, though she often spoke of her elder sister, Lady Brandram, did not, as far as I can remember, ever mention to me the existence of Sir Hugh, who, at the time of our marriage, could only have been a youngster about ten years old."

Ursula understood it all at last. For the first time she grasped the reason of many things, but the point which was uppermost in her mind was the all-important one of her real antecedents. "I am his equal after all," she thought, "and no humbly-born country girl, as he fancied." And this idea brought balm to her self-love, which had been so mortally wounded by Sir Hugh.

"You see, Ursula," the farmer was saying, "as soon

as I learned that it was your own aunt who wanted you to go and stay with her, and take you out into society, I decided at once to send you to London, for, as Isobel's daughter, it was your birthright to take the place of a lady of position. I thought to myself, that if you should marry well, why, after all, that would be exactly what you had a right to do, being a gentlewoman born."

"It was strange," said Ursula, "that Lady Brandram should have been my friend for so long, and yet that we should never have found out our relationship."

"Not strange at all, child, because she had no clue to your identity."

"I remember now, that she always said I was very like her dead sister; but of course at the time it never struck me how deep a significance those words bore."

"It may seem strange to you that such a lady as your mother was should ever have condescended to marry a plain farmer like myself; but you see, Ursula, hers had been a life full of so much trouble that she appeared glad to come and find rest and a quiet home under my roof. It was all right in her case to come down to my level, for she was too world-worn to ever care again for a gay life. So all that love could do to make her happy she had in full," and here the old man's eyes shone with a brighter light, "for I worshipped the very ground my Isobel trod on. My thought ever was to make up to her by every means in my power for the dead years of her past. But for you, Ursula, it was different; and I sometimes think that Isobel made a mistake when she refused to let me send you to her relations. It was your right to have at least a choice in the matter."

While Mr. Harlowe was speaking, the girl had been pondering in a desultory manner on the similarity of the histories of her life and that of her mother. Both of them had weathered the storms of sombre days and darkest nights; both had married in order to gain peace and the protection of a good man against the world.

"So far no harm has come of my silence," said the old farmer, "for you did marry a good honest husband, and a gentleman to boot, my dear; and with that reflection I comfort myself every hour."

No harm! As Ursula heard Mr. Harlowe utter these words, her heart sickened at the recollection of all the misery and unspeakable wretchedness which had been her portion during so many months. No harm! when her life and love had been wrecked and shattered all because of this untold tale. Oh! the horrible irony of Fate! Now, when happiness had fled, and earthly things were all neutral-coloured, when hope and faith and sweet content were stricken low, the old man spoke the words which, had they been uttered four years before, would have altered all her cruel destiny. Had Sir Hugh Galbraith known that she was his equal, he might have loved her, wooed her, won her, and then—

"I shall write to Lady Brandram to-morrow," Ursula heard the old man saying, "and repeat what I have told you to-night. She and Sir Hugh must at once learn the story from me. I owe it to them in part justification of my long silence."

"Yes, to-morrow," murmured Ursula. Oh! the to-morrows—what could they ever bring to her but loneliness and sorrow, each one a repetition of the others. As her head sank down upon her clasped hands, the girl broke into hard, dry sobs which wrung her very heart-strings. It is always left unto women to weep for the sins of men.

CHAPTER III.

"The tender grace of a day that is dead,
Will never come back to me."

—TENNYSON.

AND so, at last, the secret which for the space of twenty years had been securely locked up in the heart of old Mr. Harlowe was kept inviolate no longer. It was a strange story which he had told to Ursula in the fire-light on that dark December night, and yet one so simple as to be no uncommon tale of events. The whole thing fitted together perfectly, like a child's map, and the whys and wherefores had their answers in the facts laid down just as they actually happened.

Naturally it gave Ursula much food for thought. Not for one moment did she blame the farmer for withholding from her the knowledge that she was the Honourable Ursula Wyvern, and not Miss Harlowe of Deepdene Farm; for she was devotedly attached to him, and that her mother had implored his silence upon the subject was to the girl an all-sufficient justification for the course he had pursued.

Mr. Harlowe carried out his intention of writing a full account of the life of Isobel Mornington to her sister, Lady Brandram. But the letter which he addressed to Sir Hugh upon the same subject, lay for several days at "White's," unclaimed by its owner, for

Galbraith, having taken a short run down into Essex, with the full expectation of returning to London in a couple of days, had not left any directions with regard to the forwarding of his letters. Consequently, when a sudden determination seized upon him to go to Deepdene and see Ursula, he started for Arleton in complete ignorance of the revelations which had been made by Mr. Harlowe, both to his aunt and himself, through the medium of the post.

The baronet had not seen Mrs. Comstock for nearly a year, and each day since he had heard of her husband's death he became more and more desirous of once more seeking the presence of the only woman he had ever loved. A certain respect for her recent bereavement restrained his impatience for a time, but, at length, a longing took such strong possession of him to look upon her dear face again, to hear the sound of her voice, and to feel the clasp of her hand, that, bidding an abrupt farewell to the friends with whom he was staying, Sir Hugh whirled away, as swiftly as steam could convey him, to the little Herefordshire village.

During the past three years Galbraith had not permitted himself even to think of Ursula, far less to see her except very occasionally, for he feared from the depths of his heart, that, if he voluntarily retained her personality in his mind, some further terrible disaster might occur, as the consequence of his unfathomable power. Therefore he had cut himself off, as much as possible, from all intercourse, either direct or indirect, with the girl, from the moment in which he learned that she was another man's wife. Now, however, all was changed, and the baronet firmly believed that, as there had been no demonstration of the existence of his unconscious hypnotic power for so long a period, the force (whatever it was) must be dead.

The snow lay thick upon the ground, and the distant hills were blotted out by heavy banks of clouds piled high up into the leaden-coloured sky. It was about three o'clock in the afternoon of New Year's day when Galbraith alighted at Arleton Station, and at once engaged a trap to convey him out to Deepdene.

Mr. Harlowe was honestly glad to see the baronet again, and bade him heartily welcome, insisting that he should remain for at least one night under the roof of the farm-house.

"Of a surety you can spare us one day," said the old man cheerfully; but Sir Hugh only gave him an evasive answer, for the young man knew well in his own heart that it rested with Ursula to decide whether he should go or stay.

"Thanks, Mr. Harlowe. I will see how the evening turns out; but if it is fine I think it may be best for me to make my way back to the 'Arms,' in order to catch the early morning train up to Town."

"Well, well, we'll see. Maybe you can stay though,

and Ursula will be glad of your company, I make no doubt. It is but a lonely life for the lass down here, with me out all day in the open."

As he thus rambled on in hospitable vein, he led Sir Hugh across the hall into the oak parlour, and, throwing wide the door, said:

"Ursula, here is a visitor."

The girl turned her head at the sound of the farmer's voice, and, looking up, encountered the baronet's gaze fixed upon her, as he paused for an instant upon the threshold of the room.

"Sir Hugh!" she cried in surprise, and rising with a slow dignity, which was the acquisition of recent years, she came towards him and held out a friendly hand in greeting.

"Yes, Mrs. Comstock, it is really I. You see I have taken the liberty of paying you a very informal visit."

"I am glad to see you," said Ursula; and, as she uttered the stereotyped phrase, she felt painfully conscious of how bald the words were; yet at the same time she experienced a total inability to conjure up any warmer speech of welcome.

Mr. Harlowe made up for all her deficiencies, however, by his good-natured commonplaces, for he remarked on the weather, the condition of the roads and the state of agriculture, in such an easy, unconcerned manner that it considerably helped out the conversation, and was a vast relief to the two other participants. No allusion was made to Ursula's story, and yet two out of the three persons congregated round the hearth were horribly conscious of it all the time they spoke only on extraneous topics.

Presently the old man got up, saying that he had something to attend to.

"I must leave you for an hour, Sir Hugh; but Ursula will entertain you, and after supper we can have a smoke and a talk together. Of course, you got my letter last week?"

"What letter, Mr. Harlowe?"

"Why the one I sent to your club on Tuesday."

"No, I have not yet received it. The fact is, I have been in Essex for a few days, and left no directions for the forwarding of my mail."

"Ah!" broke from Ursula involuntarily, "then you do not know—"

"The contents of your father's letter, Mrs. Comstock? No, I do not; but surely it will not matter much, for now we can talk things over, and that will be much more satisfactory."

Ursula and Mr. Harlowe exchanged glances.

"It was about an important business," remarked the farmer, "but as there is a somewhat long story connected with it, we will leave all discussion until this evening." With which sentence he left the room and its occupants to dead silence.

There was a long, awkward pause. Ursula was staring into the fire and tapping one foot monotonously on the fender-rail, her thoughts meandering in a disconnected sort of way from subject to subject. It was strange, she pondered, that the presence of the man she had once adored so passionately should not now have the power to make her pulses even quicken or to awaken one spark of ardent feeling within her breast. In these reflections the girl did not make any allowance for the long separation which was the direct cause of the weakening of his unconscious hypnotic influence over her; for naturally, she being in total ignorance of the fact that Sir Hugh had ever exercised any force over her, could not guess that the circumstance of her affection for him having died, was perhaps not the real reason why the baronet failed to stir up any reciprocal warmth in her heart.

The truth was that the man's marvellously developed power over her was lessened by reason of their long separation, just as conscious hypnotic influence is weakened by disuse. But Ursula fancied that because her affection for him was non-existent, he would never again be able to exercise any control over her. How unfounded this conclusion was, subsequent events indisputably showed.

Sir Hugh sat on the opposite side of the hearth, oppressed with the dumbness which so frequently kills all words upon the tongue of a man when he is in the presence of the woman he loves.

It was very unfortunate, thought the girl, that her cousin should have come to Deepdene in entire ignorance of the relationship which was now known to exist between them; it made such a tremendous difference in their relative positions. All at once Galbraith recovered his powers of speech.

"Mrs. Comstock," he began, "there is something I want to say to you, but before I can explain myself fully, I shall have to speak of an event which took place more than three years ago."

Ursula, sharply recalled to the present by his earnest words, began to wonder what second revelation was going to be sprung upon her. She bowed quietly, and Sir Hugh continued:

"I have no excuse to offer for the grievous wrong I once did to you. What happened in those by-gone months can never be cancelled now; all I dare hope or plead for is that you will allow that period of our intercourse to be buried in oblivion. Can you do this for me? Will you forget, even if you cannot forgive, my mad folly and wickedness in attempting to experiment with you? The man stood up as he spoke, and leaned with one elbow upon the mantlepiece, his face pale with suppressed emotion.

"I forgave you long ago, Sir Hugh," said Ursula gravely; "do not let us rake up that old episode again."

The baronet's muscles relaxed. "You do not yet understand what this particular assertion of yours means to me," he said slowly. "I can now go on to tell you of what occurred immediately after your marriage to your late husband; but had you still harboured feelings of anger or resentment against me, justifiable as I must admit they would have been, I should have been debarred forever from asking you to——but I must begin at the beginning."

"The beginning of what?"

"Of the story I am now going to tell you."

"A story!"

"Yes, the story of my love."

"I do not quite comprehend. Who—"

"Who was my love? Is that what you would ask me? Oh! Mrs. Comstock—Ursula—" as he took a step towards her, "can you not guess that it is of you alone I am speaking? You were and are and will be my only love on earth," and with an involuntary gesture he held out his arms in the direction of the woman he was addressing.

She could scarcely believe her ears.

"Sir Hugh, this is absurd!" she exclaimed. "You barely tolerated me in the old days. What new freak of yours is this with which you are trying to play upon my feelings?"

"As there is a God above us, I swear it is the truth. The knowledge of all that you really were to me struck me like a flash of lightning on that awful morning when I saw you in Comstock's house, the bride of an hour, another man's wife." He paused, strangled for an instant by the recollection of that terrible meeting.

Ursula moved restlessly. This was all so unexpected and so strange; but as yet his words did not stir her very deeply.

"I knew in that moment that I loved you," Galbraith went on; "you brought to light all the passionate feelings of which I was capable,—and Ursula," here his tone sank, "I have loved you from a distance ever since. Darling, will you not love me a little too?"

"Sir Hugh," cried the girl, drawing back; "you must really be mad to talk like this."

"No," he replied, "I am as sane as any man in love ever is. See,—I lay my heart at your feet,—will you trample on it so unmercifully? You are the cold one now, dearest; our positions are reversed."

"Yes, they are, indeed. Do you know who I am? But, of course you do not. I am Ursula Comstock, formerly Ursula Wyvern, the daughter of your aunt, Lady Wyvern, by her first marriage, and — your own cousin."

As she proudly uttered these sentences, the girl rose and stood confronting Galbraith with flaming eyes and head thrown back. The hot words on the baronet's tongue died away in amazement at her statement, so clear and concise that it never struck him to doubt its truth.

"How?"—he began, and then stopped. "Why did you never tell me this before? Why did you deceive us all?"

Then she told him the story of her mother's life, and of the dying woman's request that it might be kept a secret as long as possible.

"Surely all you have repeated to me need not make any difference between us," said Galbraith, as she paused. "I told you that I loved you before I heard all this wonderful story, and I tell you again that I love you just the same,—not one whit less, or one whit more, for the altered circumstances of your birth. Ursula, will you marry me?"

"No, I will never marry you, Sir Hugh."

"But—"

"Stay a moment; I want to tell you that long ago I loved you, too, my cousin. Ah! you look surprised, but it is true, and I feel no shame in confessing it openly now. I loved you with all my fresh young heart and soul—and you—you, Sir Hugh Galbraith, scorned the little country girl as a child beneath your notice. Do not protest," as she held up a warning hand to check the words which trembled on his lips; "it is my turn to speak now. You will never be loved again as I loved you in those dear, dead days. I was yours, body and soul, and I worshipped you as only a woman can worship the man she believes in and trusts to the limit of life itself. You were my hero then—chivalrous—honourable—perfect—as no other man was ever perfect in my eyes before—for I loved you, Hugh, and in the light of my adoration I saw nothing but your noblest qualities. My love was so beautiful in itself that it enveloped you in a reflected glamour, until—the blackness of disillusionization darkened its brilliancy. Now all is changed, and you come to me to sue for what is no longer mine to give."

She paused wearily, and the lines in her face seemed curved with the impress of sorrow.

"But, Ursula, if you loved me then, surely you love me a little still?" he pleaded.

"No," she replied, sitting down in the big armchair again; "I do not love you, simply because I have lost the power to love anyone."

The girl felt exhausted, wearied of the past and the present, and too tired to care about the future.

"Darling," said Galbraith, as he dropped on to one knee beside her, "do not be so cruel. Was it only in order to tantalize that you have just told me how much you cared for me in those old days?"

"I do not wish to be unnecessarily cruel. But you made me suffer then—ah! more than human nature could bear, and now in your royal way you come to demand——."

"No, no, Ursula, you wrong me there. I own that I treated you shamefully once; but, darling, I love you now," and, as he spoke, Galbraith laid his hand upon hers, and forced her to look up at him. "I love you. Give me a little hope?"

"I cannot," she replied; but even as she uttered the words the girl felt her voice quiver.

Sir Hugh was looking full into her eyes, and, while he thus held her attention, she began to tremble and sway a little. It was only a flicker of the old domination of his gaze, but it frightened her, faint as it was, and with an effort she wrenched her eyes away from his face and stared blankly at the floor.

"Dearest," he murmured, "think for a moment; is there no tiny gleam of hope for me in the future?"

"There is none," she replied unfalteringly; for as soon as she had conquered the momentary influence, the girl slowly sank again into a state of utter indifference which made her callous to the crushingness of her words.

"You are so hard," he urged. "You have changed, Ursula. Is all your old gentleness dead?"

"For you? Yes."

"And your eyes are cold, my sweet—their tender light has vanished."

"You blotted it out years ago," she answered, with a flash of returning animation. "You made me what I am—a woman with no feeling, no power to care for anyone or anything. Almost I could thank you for having done so; it saves one from all burning misery of heart, for now I have no heart left to trouble me with its aching: and yet again I——."

"Ursula, Ursula, do not talk like that. Each word you say cuts me to the quick."

"I cannot help it. I suppose I do seem harsh to you; but Hugh, I do not mean to be unkind. I am just indifferent, that is all."

"All!" he cried, fiercely flinging away her hand, which until then he had held tightly in his own. "All! Is it not enough—and too much? Oh! you women, how hard you can be. Talk of forgiveness—why, you do not even know the meaning of the word.

You prate of forgetting, condoning, and all the time you hurl crushing avalanches of punishment on a man's head. Do you think I shall believe that you ever loved me, when you can sit there like an iceberg, that scornful, steely look upon your face? Love—passion—what do you know of them? What do you know of the burning torrent of lava that rushes through a man's veins when he loves a woman? Bah! Is this your revenge?"

"No, I never thought of such a thing," she cried protestingly, roused by his accusing words; "but you treated me like a puppet, Hugh, and now that you find I am human, you are angry. Ah! my cousin, perhaps your fever of love will pass away as mine did; but I pray that you may never be left as desolate as I am to-day. Wait a moment" as he tried to interrupt her; "you must know in your heart that great as my love for you was, so far, far greater, is my loss now—loss of faith in the spirit of chivalry, and loss of belief in the humanity of men. You spared nothing to heighten the cruelty of my martyrdom, and therefore ——"

"Forgive me, Ursula; I should not have accused you so unjustly; but, darling, I am not responsible for all I say. You are right," he added, humbled in an instant by the truth of her words; "I deserve all your reproaches, and many more than you can ever cast upon me; but will you not exercise a woman's right of pardoning? I am conscious now of only one desire—to win you. Dearest, look up at me. My love, give yourself to me; let me take you in my arms to cherish for the rest of our lives. Sweetheart, think of what it would mean, just you and I always together, the past blotted out, the future one long dream of pleasure. Forgive, and love me, my darling; see, I ask it on my knees." And as he pleaded Galbraith threw his whole soul into his words.

Once again he was looking at the girl with nothing but love and entreaty in his eyes; and as she slowly turned and saw him kneeling thus, she flung out her hands towards him, and for an instant appeared upon the point of relenting, when he suddenly spoke again.

"Give me just one ray of hope that some day you will come to me? What can I say, oh! what can I say? All words sound so cold I cannot tell you one quarter of my deep passionate love for you, my sweet."

And all the while he pleaded the girl grew more softened, seemingly impressed by the deep tenderness of his words.

"I am no boy, but a man," went on Galbraith "with a man's full capacity to love; and you, my darling, have it all—all my heart and soul and thoughts and prayers. Can you send me away hopeless now?"

Could she? What was this delicious sense of rest that was stealing over her, soothing and calming every over-wrought faculty? Their eyes met; their hands were locked in each other's; gently the girl swayed towards him; and in another moment would have been clasped in his arms, but at that instant a sharp bark from Don startled Sir Hugh, and he turned to look at the dog, thus removing his gaze from Ursula's. At once his power over her snapped, and she tore her hands violently from his detaining grasp.

"It is no use," she said fiercely; then added sadly, "I am sorry for it all, but you see I cannot help it."

"Ah! that is always the way with a woman. She cannot understand the strength of a man's passion."

"God created us on different days, and so I suppose we never shall quite comprehend one another's natures," replied Ursula softly.

"You are so dear to me, darling, that it is 'Sweetheart, sweetheart, sweetheart,' in my thoughts all day long. Always you—of you—and for you. Often it is a relief just to say your name over and over again to myself, for it brings you nearer to me, somehow."

She stretched out her fingers, and gently stroked his strong nervous hands.

"Do not go on," she said. "I cannot bear it, and it does no good, for nothing will ever alter what I have told you."

"Is it really all at an end between us?" he asked unsteadily.

"Yes," very low.

The man saw that she meant it, and gave up the struggle.

"I can only wait then," he said, and his face was exceedingly sad. "Let us part as friends, at least. I shall not see you again for a long time."

The girl rose and held out both her hands.

"Good-bye," she murmured, "good-bye, Hugh, and her voice sounded a little choked.

"Good-bye," he answered. "God hold you in His keeping, my sweetheart." And then he went away.

CHAPTER IV.

> "They say she died; it seems to me
> That after days of pain and strife,
> She slept one evening peacefully,
> And woke in Everlasting Life."

THERE followed many days during which Sir Hugh had ample time to realize the utter futility of his experiment. The very ground-work of his scheme had been swept away when Ursula was proved beyond a doubt to be the daughter of Lord and Lady Wyvern, and her claims to social standing were successfully established, not on the frail basis of theoretical experiment, but upon the solid rock of birth-right and descent.

Retribution had indeed overtaken him with rapid strides; for what had he now to look forward to? The shattered wreck of an attempted experiment clogged his feet, whilst a hopeless passion filled his heart.

One thought alone comforted the man through the weeks succeeding his visit to Deepdene, and that was the certainty that at length he had completely lost all unconscious hypnotic force, for the baronet was fully convinced that he no longer exercised any influence whatsoever over Ursula Comstock. Her refusal to marry him confirmed this belief in his mind. Had she still been in any degree under his control, she could not, he argued, have so ruthlessly sent him away out of her life—for Sir Hugh was quite ignorant of the faint glimmer of a returning submission to his domination which the girl had experienced during their recent interview.

So he now felt entirely at liberty to think of Ursula as much as he pleased, unmolested by all fear of injuring her, and, for the first time in three years, he completely abandoned himself to the delight of picturing to his mind the woman he loved, as vividly and as often as he pleased.

For the first twenty-four hours after Sir Hugh's departure, Ursula experienced a sensation of relief, almost amounting to peace. Her love for Galbraith was dead—this she had fully proved by her refusal to marry him—and she determined to put him thenceforward out of her thoughts forever, just as she had expunged him out of her life. All went well for a day. But at the end of that time she was forced to admit that she could not altogether blot out the remembrance of him. A second day passed, and then a third—even a fourth came and went—and still she thought of him—always, too, in a nervous, strained, unnatural manner.

At the conclusion of a week the girl became so restless and excitable that Mr. Harlowe remonstrated seriously with her. She pleaded a bad headache as an excuse, but all the while was perfectly well aware that no such ordinary malady could account for her conduct. Sleep had well nigh deserted her, and she could no longer eat anything substantial. Racked and torn by this inward struggle against she knew not what, Ursula suffered intense torture day and night.

There was absolutely no physical reason for her suffering thus, yet ill she certainly was. And through it all her mind perpetually dwelt upon Sir Hugh Galbraith—not voluntarily or deliberately, but as if she were compelled to think of him by some unseen power. It was not that the girl felt any returning love for the baronet, but simply that she thought of him unceasingly, and a very tumult of conflicting emotions raged within her breast.

At last the climax came. The tired brain gave way, and Ursula Comstock succumbed to a violent attack of brain fever, which presumably was the result of the unconscious hypnotic influence exercised over her by Sir Hugh.

The only possible explanation appears to be that the baronet had, by reason of incessant telepathy, revived all his old power over the girl, and that as hour by hour he fixed his mind upon her personality, so day by day he again unconsciously hypnotized her. He could not make her love him—that was impossible—but, if it was true that he was endowed with unusual mental power, it was more than probable that he alone was responsible for Ursula's extraordinary illness.

As may be supposed, Lady Brandram was astonished beyond measure when she received Mr. Harlowe's communication and learned the true history of her niece's parentage. With the not infrequent self-satisfaction of an elderly woman, she said to herself, "I always felt sure that the girl was a lady." It is so easy to know things after they have been told to us! Her first act was to sit down and write to the young widow a long letter of kindest welcome into the Mornington family, coupled with an urgent invitation to her to visit London as soon as possible, and thus renew old friendship under a new aspect.

To this, however, the old lady, somewhat to her surprise, received no immediate answer. And nearly two weeks elapsed before any word from Deepdene reached her. When, towards the middle of January, Lady Brandram did obtain news of Ursula, it came in the sad form of a telegram, requesting her to go at once to Arleton, where her presence was urgently needed, as the girl was very ill. Without delay she started off, and within twelve hours stood by the bedside of her niece. That Ursula was dangerously ill, Lady Brandram saw at a glance. A trained nurse was summoned, and a celebrated doctor telegraphed for from Town, but before night came on the invalid was raving in all the delirium of high fever.

Days of terrible anxiety followed, during which the household moved about with noiseless tread, and hushed voices alone broke the silence that reigned in the sick-room. It was just a week since the farmer sent that hasty message calling Lady Brandram to Deepdene, and for the space of those seven days and nights Ursula had tossed and moaned upon her bed, the fever now rising, now falling slightly, as hour by hour she fought for her life.

Intervals of consciousness occurred, but they were very brief, and during all her ravings, the girl's incessant cry was "Hugh! Hugh!" Once, in a lucid moment, she begged her aunt to send for Galbraith, and this was promptly done.

One night Lady Brandram sat in the oak parlour, talking gravely to Mr. Harlowe. Outside the eerie wail of the wind sounded fitfully, and in the wide throat of the chimney a hundred voices muttered of the coming storm. Presently it burst in unreasoning fury, shaking the casements, and snapping off the ivy trails as it fled shrieking across the land. But the watchers inside heeded not the wildness of the tempest.

The London physician had left the farm-house that afternoon. He could do nothing more, he said; the case was hopeless; and so he departed, taking with him the last faint ray of comfort from those who remained behind.

"While there is life there is hope," said the farmer seeming to find balm in the old phrase.

"Yes," replied Lady Brandram, "But—" and her look expressed the remainder of the sentence.

"Of course I know Brutton's opinion is the best that can be got; still, no one is infallible."

"That is true, and Dr. Craven refuses to give up entirely yet. He is going to stay here all night."

"He may be only a young country practitioner, but he is a trump all the same, and will pull my little girl through if anyone can," said Mr. Harlowe.

"You sent the telegram?"

"To Sir Hugh? Yes. He will be here by mid-day to-morrow, for I take it he will start at once."

"Most certainly. I am only sorry that I did not wire for him before. Almost the first conscious words Ursula spoke this afternoon were a request that he might be summoned. She seems to want to see him very particularly."

"Do you think she knows the—the—"

"Yes," sighed Lady Brandram, "I am sure that she does. I fancy she read it in my face, for when she asked for Hugh, the poor girl said: 'I want him to come at once, or it may be too late.'"

True to Lady Brandram's expectations, Galbraith arrived the next morning. His quiet, steady manner covered a terrible anxiety, and when in brief words his aunt told him that Ursula had but a short time to live—only a few hours perhaps—the man grew ghastly white. A slight dilation of the nostrils, and a faint quiver of the eyelids at first alone betrayed his agitation. As he began to grasp the situation, great beads of perspiration came out upon his forehead, where the veins showed like whip-cords.

" It cannot be true!" he cried. "Something must be done at once."

" Listen, Hugh," rejoined Lady Brandram, laying a restraining hand upon his arm ; " everything is being done that medical skill and nursing can accomplish. You must be calm, or I dare not let you see her."

". All right, aunt ; I can control myself," he replied, and a look of stern resolve instantly masked his features.

The baronet spent all that afternoon in the sick room. His presence had soothed the dying girl, and as she lay there, perfectly conscious, but too weak to do much more than smile at him, a deep sweet peace fell upon her tired brain, and she was at rest. As evening came on, Ursula asked that the curtains should be drawn aside in order that she might see the snow-laden trees, and the sky where the glorious colour-changes of a winter sunset were sobering into nothingness. The supreme reign of night was fast setting in, and as she gazed upon the tender grey-blue harmony of nature, the girl felt its beauty steal into her soul.

Ursula and Sir Hugh, alone together, watched the light slowly die out in the western horizon. The girl's fingers were clasped in his, and her face was turned towards him.

" My darling," he murmured gently, passing his disengaged hand over her forehead.

She looked at the man as he spoke—looked deep

down into those fathomless eyes which had taught her all the awful lore of Love and Sorrow.

Gently he drew her slight frame towards him, until her head rested upon his shoulder.

"I feel better, Hugh," she said.

"Because you are in my arms, my sweet ?"

"I do not know, but I seem stronger somehow. Why is it ?"

"Who can tell, dearest ? Never mind the reason, as long as you are comfortable."

"I wish I could love you, Hugh," she went on, after a pause.

"What a strange remark, darling. But I think you must care for me a little, or you would not—"

"I know ; but do not misunderstand me—it is different. I seem to want you, to be with you—but, Hugh," very earnestly, "it is not love."

Galbraith pressed her hands gently.

"I do not understand it myself," she continued.

"Do not try to, sweetheart."

Then followed a long interval, fraught with perfect rest to the girl, and deepest sorrow to the man.

"Are you tired, dearest ?" he asked presently.

"A little," came the soft reply.

Alas ! He knew that she was dying. But what he did not know was that exhausted nature had at last yielded to the sapping power of his Unconscious Hypnotism.

She was quite ready to go. At peace with the

world, her friends around her,—she asked for nothing more. Death did not seem hard—it was only a going beyond the stars after all.

The girl lay back upon the pillows, her eyes still turned to the west. Fainter and fainter grew the glow left by the now vanished sun. Darker and darker loomed the shadows that stole from out the corners of the room.

"Hold me, Hugh!"

The cry came sharp and sudden.

The man bent over her, a terrible fear gripping his heart.

"Shall I call Aunt Mary?" he asked quickly.

"No," she was lying quite still again. "I just want you beside me." And she closed her eyes.

The gloom increased, and as Galbraith watched by her, praying in his heart, as he had never prayed in all his life before, a star shone out in the darkening sky.

Was it the sign that a soul had been newly carried up to Heaven?

As Sir Hugh knelt on beside the lifeless form of Ursula, the mighty echo of an unanswered, unanswerable question rolled down the Avenues of Time—WAS SHE HYPNOTIZED?

THE END.

www.ingramcontent.com/pod-product-compliance
Lightning Source LLC
Chambersburg PA
CBHW030341270326
41926CB00009B/913
* 9 7 8 3 7 4 4 7 2 4 9 6 8 *